LUTHER
A GUIDE FOR THE PERPLEXED

T&T Clark *Guides for the Perplexed*

T&T Clark's Guides for the Perplexed are clear, concise and accessible introductions to thinkers, writers and subjects that students and readers can find especially challenging. Concentrating specifically on what it is that makes the subject difficult to grasp, these books explain and explore key themes and ideas, guiding the reader towards a thorough understanding of demanding material.

Guides for the Perplexed available from T&T Clark

Balthasar: A Guide for the Perplexed, Rodney Howsare
Benedict XVI: A Guide for the Perplexed, Tracey Rowland
Calvin: A Guide for the Perplexed, Paul Helm
Christian Bioethics: A Guide for the Perplexed, Agneta Sutton
Christology: A Guide for the Perplexed, Alan Spence
De Lubac: A Guide for the Perplexed, David Grumett
Eucharist: A Guide for the Perplexed, Ralph N. McMichael
Pannenberg: A Guide for the Perplexed, Timothy Bradshaw
Theological Anthropology: A Guide for the Perplexed, Marc Cortez
Tillich: A Guide for the Perplexed, Andrew O'Neill
The Trinity: A Guide for the Perplexed, Paul M. Collins
Wesley: A Guide for the Perplexed, Jason E. Vickers

Forthcoming titles

Martyrdom: A Guide for the Perplexed, Paul Middleton
Political Theology: A Guide for the Perplexed, Elizabeth Philips
Process Theology: A Guide for the Perplexed, Bruce Epperly
Sin: A Guide for the Perplexed, Derek Nelson

LUTHER
A GUIDE FOR THE PERPLEXED

DAVID M. WHITFORD

t & t clark

Published by T&T Clark International
A Continuum Imprint
The Tower Building, 11 York Road, London SE1 7NX
80 Maiden Lane, Suite 704, New York, NY 10038

www.continuumbooks.com

British Library Cataloguing-in-Publication Data
A catalogue record for this book is available from the British Library

ISBN13 :   978-0-567-03278-2 (Hardback)
           978-0-567-03279-9 (Paperback)

Typeset by Newgen Imaging Systems Pvt Ltd, Chennai, India
Printed and bound in Great Britain by the MPG Books Group

For Laurel

CONTENTS

LIST OF ILLUSTRATIONS

PREFACE

In seminary, I took a class on the theology of Karl Barth. On the first day of class, the professor described Barth's theology as a great medieval cathedral. If one enters a cathedral during the daytime, the first few moments inside can be quite disorienting. You know immediately that you are inside something magnificent, but your eyes have not yet adjusted to the light. As you spend time inside and as your eyes adjust, the true glory that surrounds you slowly comes into view. The windows now explode with color and the arches seem to stretch to the heavens themselves. As I sat there that day, I thought of Cologne Cathedral. It is massive and dark and looms over the city of Cologne and the Rhein River. Inside, however, it is one of the most beautiful and splendid cathedrals I have ever been into. I have always thought that this image of a theologian as a cathedral is a wonderful image for any theologian of some complexity and depth. Each and every theologian has a particular way of thinking and writing that take some time to appreciate and understand. Even after one's eyes adjust to the dim light inside the cathedral, however, there are still a number of alcoves and corners that remain in shadows. Those shadows take much longer to investigate and understand. I hope that this book can serve as an initial tour of the cathedral-like theology of Martin Luther. Luther is much like the Cologne Cathedral. He towers over Protestantism and Protestant thought like no other theologian. As one approaches his theology and his writings, one can begin to feel particularly small. The complete collection of his writings, bible commentaries, and sayings runs nearly 100 large volumes. That amount of literature can give even the seasoned reader of theology weak knees. It does not have to be so, however. Just as the windows, arches, and aisles of a cathedral draw your eye to the center of the cathedral and up to the heavens, so too there are dominant themes and patterns of thought that run throughout Luther's theology. This book is designed to help you navigate those themes and patterns. It is my hope that as you begin to explore Luther, your eyes will adjust to the light within his thought. There are many magnificent windows and some dark corners as well. Both the brilliance of the windows and the darkness of the corners are part of who Luther was and we cannot be fair either to history or to his theology if we cast our focus on only one aspect of his life and thought and ignore the other. We will begin our tour of cathedral of his thought by looking at the world into which he was born and then at his life. We will then look at some of the most important aspects of his theology, including justification, the Law and the Gospel, and his understanding of the human will. The third section of the book moves us into beyond pure theology to consider Luther's social and political thought. Here we come to the two darkest corners of Luther's works, his writings and actions towards the peasants in the 1525 Peasants' War and his relationship to Jews and Judaism. In trying to explain and understand those dim corners, it is my hope that I have been both fair and equitable to both Luther and to those he wrote about and against.

As with any great cathedral, one visit is simply not enough to truly appreciate all that it has to offer. This book is designed to give you your initial tour into Luther's world and his theology. In each chapter you will find other resources to deepen your understanding of Luther. The best place, of course, to begin to understand Luther is to read him. Luther was not a purely academic theologian. His was an active and pastoral theologian. He wrote about life and to people. In this way, he can be immensely approachable and sometimes frustrating because he, like the rest of us, is not always consistent and he sometimes contradicts himself. All of this makes him all the more interesting and fascinating.

This book is dedicated to my wife Laurel, who is sometimes bemusedly perplexed by the amount of time that I spend working on Martin Luther. She is my Katherina von Bora. Luther married in 1525 and that relationship transformed his life for the better. My life is made better daily because of Laurel.

ACKNOWLEDGMENTS

Portions of Chapter 6 on the Antichrist were previously published in "The Papal Antichrist: Martin Luther and the Underappreciated Influence of Lorenzo Valla," *Renaissance Quarterly* 61/1 (2008): 26–52.

Portions of Chapter 7 on politics were previously published in "From Speyer to Magdeburg: The Development and Maturation of a Hybrid Theory of Resistance," *Archive for Reformation History* 96 (2005): 57–80.

I wish to thank Thomas Kraft of T&T Clark for first approaching me with this project. The chance to work on a project aimed at introducing students to Luther for perhaps the first time is one that I cherish. Anna Turton, also of T&T Clark, has been kind and patient with me as I have tried to bring this project to completion. Of course, none of this would have been possible without the support of my home institution and I wish to thank President Wendy Edwards of United Theological Seminary for encouraging this project.

As always, I could not have written this book (or anything else I work on) without the constant help and dedication of Brillie Scott, United's stupendous ILL librarian, who always manages to track down my obscure requests.

Finally, I wish to thank Carter Lindberg for being the person who was my best guide to the theological cathedral that is Martin Luther.

ABBREVIATIONS

CWE	*Collected Works of Erasmus.* Toronto: University of Toronto Press, 1974–.
DR	*Deutsche Reichstagsakten: Jüngere Reihe.* Gotha: Perthes, 1896.
LW	*Luther's Works.* Edited by H. J. Grimm and H. T. Lehmann. 55 vols. St. Louis and Philadelphia: Concordia and Fortress, 1958–1986.
PE	*Works of Martin Luther.* Philadelphia Edition. Philadelphia: Holman, 1915–1943.
WA	*D. Martin Luthers Werke: Kritische Gesamtausgabe,* 120 vols. Weimar: Bohlaus, 1883–.
WABR	*D. Martin Luthers Werke: Briefwechsel* (Letters).
WATR	*D. Martin Luthers Werke: Tischreden* (Table Talk).

PART I

INTRODUCTION TO LUTHER'S LIFE AND TIMES

CHAPTER 1

MARTIN LUTHER'S EUROPE

"Et mortuus vivit." He is dead, yet he lives. Philip Melanchthon penned the words beneath an ink drawing of Martin Luther in 1546. Luther was 63 when he died and those 63 years would have been some of the most dramatic in European history even without him. During Luther's lifetime, the printing press went from being an odd new invention to an agent of widespread change and revolution. Columbus sailed the Atlantic the year he turned 9. That same year, Ferdinand and Isabella completed their expulsion of Muslim rule in Iberia. In 1501, as Luther set off for university, Michelangelo began carving *David*. A few years later, when Luther journeyed to Rome, if he had wanted to he could have watched Michelangelo working on the Sistine Chapel ceiling. As Luther debated his new understanding of Christianity in Leipzig with Johannes Eck in 1518, Ferdinand Magellan was setting sail to circumnavigate the globe and Hernán Cortés was preparing to attack the Aztec city of Tenochtitlan. As Luther penned the three great treatises of 1520, Suleiman the Magnificent ascended to the throne of the Ottoman Empire. Just a few years before Luther died, Nicolaus Copernicus began his own revolution when he published *De revolutionibus orbium caelestium* (*On the Revolutions of the Heavenly Spheres*) (1543).

Despite all these other great accomplishments in art, literature, and science, when historians discussed the sixteenth century even a generation ago, Martin Luther stood above all the rest. He was the titan figure of the sixteenth century. And it is certainly true that in the year he died, his death was understood then and remains today the most important event of that year. His dominance of the sixteenth century is no longer quite so monolithic. Historians today understand that Luther was a part of rather than the center of a dynamic century. He was affected by his times just as much as he affected them. In this first chapter, we seek to understand the world in which Luther lived. To understand the man, one must also understand his times.

THE CHURCH

The church at the dawn of the sixteenth century is a perplexing institution because it was so full of contradictions. On the one hand, the papacy and Roman curia were corrupt institutions; largely governed by men more concerned with courtly life than church leadership. On the other hand, most people were deeply connected to their faith and popular acts of piety were widespread. Which picture accurately represents "the church"? The theological scene is similarly confusing. Theologians of the day debated the questions of authority, free will, and the significance of metaphysics to theology. Meanwhile, theologians and laity (whether highborn or low) lived in a world animated by portents of good and evil, witches and hexes, saints and protective prayers. For example, Luther's colleague in Wittenberg, Philip Melanchthon, once prevented Luther from traveling because the stars were ominous.[1] As a university professor and a man who ministered to common Christians, Luther had to try to balance and live in both of these theological worlds. At times, his writing engages in theological discourse of the highest order—for instance, his debate with Erasmus on the free will. At other times, his theology is deeply personal and applicable to daily life. Understanding Luther's audience and their concerns helps to clarify and often demystify his theology. Changes in audience, temperament, and aim also help explain some of the apparent changes in Luther's perspective.

Despite the paradoxes of late medieval church life, there were also a number of widespread commonalities. First, even while people on the local level remained fundamentally pious and strongly connected to their parish, nearly all Christians of the late medieval era recognized that the church, in "head and members," needed

---

1 Melanchthon, perhaps Lutheranism's greatest theologian after Luther was simultaneously a devoted believer in astrology.

renewal and reform. The calls for reform by John Wyclif (d. 1384) and Jan Hus (d. 1415) would lay some groundwork for Luther and affect the course of his life and the reception of his theology. Wyclif was an English theologian and professor at Oxford University. He was one of the earliest translators of the Bible into English. In 1373, he began work on his treatise *De Dominio*. Five years later, he followed *Dominio* with the treatise *De ecclesia*. In *Dominio* (*On Lordship*), Wyclif argues that the right to rule (whether civil or ecclesiastical) is given directly by God to the lord or prelate. Because it is given directly by God, God requires that the lord remain faithful to God's commands. God's requirements are made known in the Bible—this helps explain why he believed everyone needed to know what the Bible said and why he translated it into English. In *De ecclesia* (*On the Church*), he argues that because scripture does not give the church the right to hold property or wield power, it must set them down. Further, rather than focus on protecting special rights and privileges for themselves, priests should focus their attention on preaching, teaching the faith, and reforming their parishes. Prelates likewise must serve their people and not seek to be served. Because there were a number of political connections between England and Bohemia during the late fourteenth century, Wyclif's theology was known and discussed there. Jan Hus, a professor in Prague, found in Wyclif a theological mentor. Many of Hus's ideas on the church and the need for reform echo Wyclif. Unlike Wyclif, however, Hus did not have the unflinching support of the crown. When the church summoned him to appear before the Council of Constance in 1414, Hus naturally feared for his life. Surprisingly however, he was guaranteed safe-conduct to the Council by the Holy Roman Emperor, Sigismund. His welfare ensured; he traveled to Constance to defend his theology. When he arrived, he did not find a discussion but a trial. Found guilty of heresy, he was handed over to civil authorities and—despite his safe-conduct pledge—was burned at the stake. Sigismund claimed that he did not need to honor a pledge given to a heretic. When, a century later, Martin Luther received a similar summons and guarantee he walked to Worms with much less naïveté regarding his fate.

Not all calls for reform ended at the stake, however. One of the more successful late medieval reform movements took place within monastic orders. All monastic orders have a foundational set of rules or governing principles. Over time, many monasteries relaxed the rules and changed their standards. The Observant Movement called on monasteries to return to stricter observance of their founding principles. Martin Luther joined an observant monastery in Erfurt in 1505. It was within an Observant system of rigorous devotion to God and right living that Luther received some of his most importanttheological training. In many ways, as we shall see in the chapters that follow, his theological system is both an

Figure 1.1 "Four Horsemen of the Apocalypse," Albrecht Dürer, 1498. Taken from *The Work of Dürer: Reproduced in over Four Hundred Illustrations* (New York: Brentano's, 1907), p. 176.

outgrowth of this rigorist approach to Christianity and a reaction against it.

A second commonality among many late medieval Christians was a belief that they were living in the very last days before Christ returned in final judgment. For nearly a century, Europe had been suffering under a veritable cavalcade of natural and human-made disasters. Massive crop losses, plague, infestation, war, and schism convinced many that they were truly living in the last days and that the Four Horsemen of the Apocalypse had been let loose on the world (Figure 1.1). Luther was among those who believed the end of days had arrived. This informed much of the urgency he brought to theological disputes and helps explain his perspective on the Antichrist.

The church in the sixteenth century was, in many ways, very similar to any large corporate body today. It had places of vitality and places of lethargy, pockets of reform and pockets of corruption. When Luther's initial critique of indulgences arrived at the doorstep of many churchmen they did not see a revolution in the making. They saw another in a long line of discussions and debates over reform and revitalization. The church had weathered many other such diatribes; it would survive this one as well. Why it did not, at least in a solitary fashion, will be discussed in the chapters that follow.

THE POLITICAL WORLD

In 1508, "Fr. Martinus lüder de Mansfelt" was transferred from the Augustinian monastery in Erfurt to the monastery in Wittenberg. He went there to begin teaching. Though he would leave occasionally and for different reasons, for the most part he would spend most of the rest of his life there and Wittenberg would become synonymous with Luther. That he went to Wittenberg to teach rather than Leipzig or any number of other schools greatly affected the course of the Reformation. Wittenberg was (and still is) a small city in Central Germany along the banks of the Elbe River. It is less than a mile from the one side to the other and the central road runs from the castle to river. Most importantly for Luther, Wittenberg was a part of Electoral Saxony and was the location of the Duke of Saxony's most cherished creation—the new University of Wittenberg. Frederick III, often called "the Wise," established the university in 1502 as a rival to the older and more prestigious University of Leipzig, which was in his cousin and rival's land. Frederick's devotion to the university and his position as one of the seven electors of the Holy Roman Empire helped ensure Luther's survival.

The Holy Roman Empire dominated all of Central Europe in the sixteenth century. Unlike the kingdoms of France or even England, however, it lacked a strong and unified central government. The empire had a leader, but that leader's ability to control the empire was greatly hampered by the power and authority of the empire's great lords—Frederick III primary among them. For nearly all of young Martin Luther's life, the empire had been led by Maximilian I (1459–1519; r. 1493). Maximilian was the head of the Habsburg dynasty and a titan figure in his own right. His family ascended to the imperial throne two generations earlier. The imperial throne does not automatically transfer from father to son but emperors worked to ensure that their sons would succeed them. Maximilian's hopes in this regard were dashed in 1506 when his son Philip died of typhoid fever. In 1506, Maximilian remained vigorous and unassailable. However, as he grew older, imperial politics surrounding succession became fodder for intrigue and machination.

The selection of a new Holy Roman Emperor was governed by the Golden Bull of 1356. It designated seven electors. Three of the electors (or Kurfürsten) were prelates—the archbishops of Mainz, Trier, and Cologne. Four electors were great lords—the king of Bohemia, the Count Palatine of the Rhine, the Duke of Saxony, and the Margrave of Brandenburg. Together they selected the next emperor, often even before the current occupant was dead his successor was elected "King of the Romans." However, Philip's death and the fact that his oldest son, Charles (1500–1558), was still a teenager when Maximilian's health began to decline meant that succession by a Habsburg was certainly not assured and was perhaps even unlikely. The uncertainty of the impending election made the position of elector even more coveted. One who coveted the position was Albrecht Hohenzollern. Albrecht was the younger brother of the Margrave of Brandenburg and in 1513 at the age of 23 was already archbishop of Magdeburg. The addition of another elector within the family would significantly increase the family's influence and power. Such an opening occurred in February 1514 when Archbishop Uriel of Mainz died. No prelate could hold two archbishoprics simultaneously, however, and so Albrecht's desire to ascend to the

See of Mainz, and its electoral dignity, required special permission from the pope. In order to pay for the *pallium* (or seal of office) and dispensation from Leo X, Albrecht borrowed money from the House of Fugger. In order to repay the loans, Leo gave Albrecht permission to sell indulgences within his territories. One indulgence seller hired by Albrecht, Johannes Tetzel helped inspire Martin Luther's ire in 1517 and his *Ninety-Five Theses* were written in part because of Luther's disgust with Tetzel. Albrecht may have sought the position of archbishop and elector even if the future election were a *fait accompli*, the Elector of Mainz was the imperial chancellor.[2] Likewise, Luther may have (indeed already had) found other issues that raised his theological ire. However, it was the confluence of these events and the money raised by indulgences that helped propel a set of lecture and debate theses into a clarion call for reform.

If the unique makeup of the empire and the way it selected a new leader helped bring about Luther's ultimate break with Rome, it also helped keep him alive and provided him with a podium from which to continue writing and speaking. In 1519, Maximilian died. Despite all the intrigue surrounding the forthcoming election, in the end his 19-year-old grandson Charles was elected to replace him. By 1519, the so-called Luther Affair was already a factor in imperial politics. He was also the faculty star at the University of Wittenberg. We are not entirely sure of Frederick III's beliefs regarding the indulgence controversy, but we do know that he liked the fame that Luther was bringing to Wittenberg. He was also a jealous defender of German rights and privileges—especially when they came into conflict with Rome. Thus, before he agreed to cast his vote on behalf of Charles, he extracted a number of pledges from the young prince. The *Wahlkapitulation*—or election agreement—protected the authority and privileges of the great lords from imperial intrusion. They also ensured that Luther would be given a fair hearing in Germany before ever being sent for trial to Rome. Fulfilling this agreement in part, Charles granted Luther safe passage to the 1521 imperial diet (or parliament) which was then meeting in Worms. At the end of a contentious appearance before the emperor, Luther was allowed to leave the city unmolested. Later in life, Charles regretted honoring

---

2 He cast the last and deciding vote in elections and chaired their common meetings so it was a plum position.

the safe passage agreement. However, that is the regret of a seasoned and powerful statesman who had in many ways forgotten the insecurity and unease with which his younger self presided over the empire. At just 21, Charles was not yet confident enough in his authority to have challenged a lesser noble of the rank, wealth, power, and prestige of Frederick III. Frederick's protection of Luther would continue for the next four years, until his death in 1525. He was replaced by the almost equally impressive John the Constant, his younger brother. For his entire life after his papal excommunication, Martin Luther lived under the protection of the electors of Saxony. Their power and prestige within the empire kept him safe. Though at times it looked as though the emperor might make an attempt to seize him, each and every time something rose up to thwart the emperor's plan. Luther died in 1546 while still living under the protection of the Saxon elector. Within the year, however, an older, wiser, and more powerful emperor would finally reach out and attempt to crush Luther's reforms. He would eventually fail, again in part because of the divided nature of the empire. Had Luther been born in a place like England or if he had gone to teach at Leipzig instead of Wittenberg, his fortunes and the fortunes of the Reformation might have been dramatically different.

WAR

In the sixteenth century, wars of greater and lesser significance were a constant presence. The trajectory and participants in the various wars of the sixteenth century greatly affected the expansion, popularity, reception, and legality of religious reforms initiated by Luther. Quite literally, there was rarely a year in the entire long sixteenth century that did not have troops moving to or from battle. It is impossible to list all of the major engagements let alone the small conflagrations. However, a number of the most significant must be discussed because of their influence on Luther either directly or on the fortunes of his movement.

The major military powers of the sixteenth century were the Habsburg dynasty, the Ottoman Empire, and the French. When Charles Habsburg was elected Holy Roman Emperor in 1519, he already ruled a vast, rich, and powerful empire. He was the sole male heir for both of his grandfathers. From Ferdinand of Aragon and Charles's mother Joanna of Castile, he inherited the crown of

Spain, lands in Italy, and an ever-expanding empire in the Americas.[3] From Maximilian, he inherited the Duchy of Burgundy, the Low Countries, and a number of other small principalities. When the Holy Roman Empire was added to his responsibilities, he ruled over the largest amount of land and people ever. An empire that vast, however, needed to be constantly defended.

Charles's eastern frontier bordered the Ottoman Empire. The "Turkish threat" of the fifteenth and sixteenth centuries was nearly constant and flamed many of the apocalyptic visions of the age. In May 1453, the Ottoman Empire conquered the city of Constantinople. This did more than simply end the Byzantine Empire; it was a blow to the psyche of Christendom. Constantinople was founded more a thousand years earlier by the great Roman Emperor Constantine himself. Constantine had brought Christianity to the Roman world. In 1453, the last Byzantine emperor died defending the city. For the next 100 years, Christianity seemed to be in full or partial retreat against the encroachments of the Ottomans. A number of these encroachments directly affected Luther. In 1521, Charles V not only had to deal with the Luther Affair but also had to deal with the fact that Ottoman troops were approaching Belgrade. The Diet of Worms ended in May; Belgrade fell to Suleiman in August. Though Belgrade was outside the empire, its capitulation concerned almost everyone because it was yet another major city on the Danube to fall. The need to keep the powerful Frederick the Wise as an ally in the face of Ottoman aggression had to have been before the emperor and his advisors as he heard Luther's appeal. In 1526, as the imperial diet was meeting in Speyer to consider the Luther Affair, the Kingdom of Hungary fell to the Ottomans at the Battle of Mohács. The Ottomans were now on the border of the empire. In 1530, the Diet of Augsburg was called to deal with the recent siege of Vienna. For Charles, the best way to meet the Turkish threat was to secure internal unity. Religious discord and internal political fraction were not the foundations upon which he could hope to lay a successful campaign against the "invading infidel." By 1530, there were a large number of pro-Lutheran princes within the empire who did not wish to be perceived as undermining the unity of the empire in the face of the "enemy," but

---

3 He would rule much of Spain jointly with his mother. Her mental incapacity meant that for all intents and purposes, Charles ruled. He did so largely through proxies.

were also unwilling to abandon their religious convictions. The solution to this quandary would guide Protestant thought and polemics for the next 35 years: religious diversity did not undermine loyalty to the empire. For example, in 1532, Charles and the newly designated "Protestant" princes sealed the Peace of Nuremberg, which granted a cessation of anti-Protestant activities in order to unify the empire against the Turks. Here the Protestants gave living testimony to their doctrine of unity amid religious diversity by sending more money and men to the emperor's cause than had been requested.[4]

Charles not only faced constant incursion from the east, but also on his southern and western borders as well. There the antagonist was always France. In January of 1515, the 21-year-old, Francis of Angoulême became king of France. His cousin, Louis XII did not have any sons and so the throne fell to Francis the next closest male heir and Louis's son-in-law. When Charles Habsburg became Holy Roman Emperor in 1519, Francis found himself surrounded on all sides by Habsburg dominions. Already in the late fifteenth century, the Spanish kingdoms had attempted to slice off portions of southern France, and now with Burgundy, the empire, Spain, and Italy all belonging to Charles, Francis had reason to worry that he would be swallowed up in a new and massive Hapsburg empire. Over the next 30 years, Francis and Charles would spar militarily numerous times. Often their battles were focused on Italy. In 1521–1522, they fought a campaign in the Swiss territories and northern Italy. In 1527, Charles again invaded Italy because of French interference. His troops occupied Rome and sacked the city.[5] A brief settlement between Francis and Charles in 1529 at Cambrai allowed Charles to focus on Protestants before the Turks interfered again. That armistice was short lived and France and Charles continued to fight throughout the 1530s. In 1544, Charles managed to march within the vicinity of

---

4 Hajo Holborn, *A History of Modern Germany: The Reformation* (New York: Alfred A. Knopf, 1973), 217–18.

5 Though not directly connected to Luther, this occupation did have a tremendous impact of the future of the Reformation in England. Henry VIII's appeal for an annulment of his marriage to Catherine of Aragon arrived in Rome just after Charles's troops. When Henry's appeal arrived, Pope Clement VII was Charles's prisoner. As might be expected, Charles would not countenance the dishonor implied in annulling his aunt's marriage to Henry. The appeal was rejected and Henry was forced to seek another solution for his marital problems.

Paris and forced Francis to the treaty table. In the Peace of Crépy, Francis pledged to support Charles in calling for General Church Council that would resolve the Protestant question and swore not to enter into any alliances with the Protestant princes against Charles. As the conference at Crépy closed, Pope Paul III called for a council to meet in Trent in 1545. Things were finally moving in Charles's direction and he finally had a free hand to deal with the Luther Affair. By 1547, Luther was dead and Charles had defeated the Protestant princes in the Schmalkaldic War. Even then, however, it was a Pyrrhic victory. Almost as soon as Charles had vanquished the Protestant princes, a number of his allies within the empire (now fearing a vastly more powerful emperor) revolted. Likewise, France (now ruled by Henry II) abandoned the Peace of Crépy, came to aid of the revolting princes, and invaded Italy again.

In order to secure his empire against attacks by the Turks and the French, Charles V was finally forced to enter into a peace treaty with Protestant lords. In the 1555 Peace of Augsburg, Protestantism was legalized within the empire. The political doctrine of *cuius regio; ius religio* (he who rules; his religion) was solidified. Basically, *cuius regio; ius religio* meant that whoever ruled a particular estate within the empire—Saxony, for example—would determine the religious makeup of that estate. Those who did not align themselves with that region's religious outlook had to leave. The solidification of *cuius regio*, allowed Luther's reforms to survive as a legal option in the sixteenth century. Had Charles V, grandson of Their Most Catholic Majesties Ferdinand and Isabella, not been constantly plagued by warfare on multiple fronts he might well have devoted much more of his attention much earlier to stamping out Luther's innovations in theology.[6]

---

6 In 1521, at the close of the Diet of Worms, Charles reflected on his position, Luther, and his ancestors: "You know that I am descended from the most Christian emperors of the noble German nation, from the Catholic kings of Spain, the archdukes of Austria and the dukes of Burgundy . . . I am determined to support everything that these predecessors and I myself have kept . . . For it is certain that a single friar errs in his opinion which is against all of Christendom and according to which all of Christianity will be and will always have been in error both in the past thousand years and even more in the present. For that reason, I am absolutely determined to stake on this cause my kingdoms and seigniories, my friends my body and blood, my life and soul." *Deutsche Reichstagsakten*, II: 594–6, English Translation in Oscar Thulin, *A Life of Luther* (Philadelphia, PA: Fortress Press, 1966), 66.

SCHOLASTICISM AND HUMANISM

First at Erfurt and then in Wittenberg, Luther was exposed to and influenced by both Nominalism and Humanism. Traces of these influences can be seen throughout his life and in his theology. Some of the differences that he had with his opponents and even sometimes his allies can be better understood if we understand the schools of thought that influenced Luther and those with whom he debated and dialoged.

Theology has always had different schools of thought. At times these schools of thought compete aggressively—for example, the debates over sin and grace between Pelagius and Augustine. At other times, theological schools of opinion live side by side; though not always comfortably or with mutual admiration—evangelical theology and postmodern theology today, for example. Even within a particular school of thought the various members and theologians in that school do not always agree—one thinks of the fierce debate between the two twentieth-century-Neo-Orthodox theologians Karl Barth and Emil Brunner in which Barth famously published a book titled, *No! An Answer to Emil Brunner.* Finally, different denominations have their own theological heritage—Lutherans still read and quote Luther, the Reformed Tradition looks to John Calvin, Methodists to John Wesley. In all these aspects, the fifteenth and sixteenth centuries were no different from the ones that preceded it or those that have followed. Before Luther introduced the new diversity of what would become Protestantism, two major schools of thought dominated theology. Humanism, less a school of thought than an approach to learning, was found in both schools. At Erfurt and Wittenberg, Luther was exposed to Nominalism or the *via moderna*, as it was and is sometimes called. Nominalism was a theological school inspired by William of Occam (c. 1285–c. 1349) and can be contrasted with Realism or the *via antiqua*. Both Nominalism and Realism are a part of Scholasticism but approach theology from different directions and their different approaches lead to very different conclusions on a number of subjects. The word scholasticism is derived from *schola* or school because it was based in the theology faculties of the growing medieval universities. It is an academic, rather than pastoral or practical, approach to theology. Perhaps the first great "Schoolman" as Scholastic theologians were sometimes called, gave the best and most lasting definition of scholastic theology. At the end of the first chapter of his *Proslogion*, St. Anselm (1033–1109) wrote "*Neque enim quaero intelligere ut credam, sed credo ut intelligam. Nam et hoc credo, quia, nisi credidero, non intelligam"* (For I do not seek to understand in order to believe, but believe in order to understand. For this I believe, I cannot understand unless I believe).[7] Generally speaking, for scholastic theologians, the most important theological task was explaining different faith beliefs in a rational framework. In order to demonstrate theology's rationality, scholasticism focused on systemizing and organizing.

The most fundamental difference between Realism and Nominalism concerns their different approaches to the philosophical idea of universals and their comfort with the idea of paradox. Realism, is most closely associated with Thomas Aquinas (1225–1274) and was expanded by Duns Scotus (1266–1308). As a school of thought, it was closely connected to the Dominican order. According to realists, "universals" are real and can be discerned and explained using reason. A universal is an ontological reality that exists beyond concrete examples of the universal—for example, there is a universal "humanness" of which all people participate, other universals could be beauty, or justice. Nominalists argued that universals were simply human constructs that help us explain similar things but do not have a separate reality beyond themselves. At issue in this debate was the limit of human reason. Nominalists were less enthusiastic about the human mind's ability to grasp truth. They were willing to live with paradox and a limited knowledge of the world.

While training for the priesthood and then the professorate, Luther encountered both schools of thought, but his professors were largely drawn from the Nominalist tradition. Ironically, it was not the differences between Nominalists and Realists that Luther reacted to or rejected. It was actually an aspect of theology on which they had a broad agreement with only small differences in focus—the ability

---

7 Anselm of Canterbury, *Opuscula beati Anselmi archiepiscopi Cantuariensis ordinis sancti benedicti* ([Strasbourg]: [Husner], c. 1496), sig. g3r. You may see the page at, http://diglib.hab.de/inkunabeln/510-12-theol-2f-1/00097. jpg. The last line was incorporated into the great compendium of Latin theological learning and biblical exegesis, the *Glossa Ordinaria*, as an explanation for Isaiah 7.9. Anselm's student, Anselm of Laon (d. 1117), helped compile the *Glossa*. The exact quote from the *Glossa* reads, "Nisi credideritis non intelligetis." *Bibliorum Sacrorum Cum Glossa Ordinaria*, 6 vols. (Venice: 1603), 4: 91.

of human beings to affect their salvation. According to Aquinas, the goal of human life is union and fellowship with God. This beatific vision is achieved when a human being cooperates with God's gift of grace and habituates (makes a habit of) an ethically virtuous life. God initiates the act of justification and salvation by giving humanity the grace to live righteously, but one must still live righteously. Many of the Ockhamists with which Luther studied learned their theology from Gabriel Biel. Biel tried to clarify for his students the movement of justification. Human beings, on their own and without God's aid or help cannot do anything to gain their salvation. However, they can strive to live the best lives that they can—he used the phrase "do what is in them [*facere quod in se est*]." God will, of course, notice this striving and look on it with kindness. This was called *congruent merit*. Congruent in this sense comes from the Latin and roughly means "to accept." Thus, God looks at this striving and accepts it as a good and commendable thing. Because God finds this work admirable, God adds a gift of grace that allows one to deepen one's commitment to God and to righteous living. This gift is called *condign merit. Condign* comes from Latin and means, "with worth." God has added his worth to humanity's actions and salvation has been achieved. Luther will reject both Aquinas and Biel on this point.

In his rejection of medieval scholastic theology and the development of a new perspective on theology, Luther depended upon a "humanist" approach to academic life generally and theological investigation specifically. Humanism was an already established approach to scholarship in the early sixteenth century. Generally speaking, humanists valued a critical judgment and intellectual curiosity. Their catch phrase was *ad fontes*—to the sources. What this meant is that it was better to read Augustine or Cicero directly rather than read a summary of their thought or a commentary upon their thought. Critical editions of classical works poured off of sixteenth-century presses. John Calvin's first publication was a critical edition of Seneca's work on clemency. The Bible, too, came under critique. New critical editions of the Latin Bible were published, but so were original language (in Hebrew and Greek) versions. Luther began to study Hebrew in 1509. He also began to study Greek and in 1516, we can see the influence of Desiderius Erasmus's Greek New Testament in the lectures Luther was giving on the book of Romans that year. Perhaps the most famous outcome in Luther's life of this approach to scripture and study comes from the opening line of the *Ninety-Five*

Theses. The first thesis reads, "Our Lord and Master Jesus Christ, when he said "Poenitentiam agite," willed that the whole life of believers should be repentance." The phrase *poenitentiam agite* comes from Latin Vulgate version of the Gospel of Matthew, 4.17. It is best translated as "do penance." What Luther noticed, however, when he read Erasmus's edition of the New Testament was that the word in Greek, *metanoiete*, does not mean "do penance" but rather connotes the idea that one should stop what one has been doing and amend one's life. Since the *Ninety-Five Theses* were an attack on indulgences and the penitential system of salvation, this change in understanding the words of Jesus was enormously important.[8]

THE PRINTING REVOLUTION

The Humanist excitement for learning and the attention scholars paid to both religious and secular works from antiquity would not have been possible without the invention of the printing press. In 1979, Elizabeth L. Eisenstein noted that the printing press created an intellectual revolution.[9] It also enabled the Protestant Reformation.[10] For example, by the year 1500 there were nearly 200 editions of Augustine published in the Holy Roman Empire. As we have already seen, Luther's approach to scripture was deeply affected by Erasmus's edition of the Greek New Testament published in 1516. In 1519, Luther would buy Erasmus's second edition of the New Testament and use it when he translated the New Testament in German. By 1535, Erasmus had published five different editions of the New Testament. Each time, he tried to correct errors uncovered by colleagues across Europe who had other manuscript copies of the Bible.

The printing press was not a completely new invention in the fifteenth century. It was, rather, perfected by the Mainz goldsmith

---

8 When Erasmus published a Latin translation together with his Greek version, he replaced *poenentiam* with *resipiscite*, which means to return to one's senses. A pre-Luther German Bible translated the phrase "Macht buß," or "do penance." When Luther translated the New Testament in 1522, he translated *metanoiete* as "Bessert euch," amend yourself.

9 Elizabeth L. Eisenstein, *The Printing Press as an Agent of Change: Communication and Cultural Transformations in Early Modern Europe*, 2 vols. (Cambridge: Cambridge University Press, 1979).

10 Mark U. Edwards, *Printing, Propaganda, and Martin Luther* (Berkeley: University of California Press, 1994); Steven E. Ozment, *Protestants: The Birth of a Revolution* (New York: Doubleday, 1992).

Johannes Gutenberg sometime in the late 1440s. Gutenberg's genius was to make metal letters that could be arranged on a block in any order, an image was then impressed with ink onto paper, and repeated. Once one had enough of that page, one could then move on to other pages by taking the letters off the board. This allowed for a rapid increase in the creation of a book. For example, in the mid-fifteenth century, the libraries at Cambridge University had less than 200 hand-copied books. By 1535, just a century later, the library at the relatively small and new University of Wittenberg had volumes in the hundreds and hundreds.

Luther had used the printing press in Wittenberg from his earliest moments as a teacher. When he lectured on the Bible, for example, he had the book under consideration printed for his students. The text of the Bible was printed down the center of the page with wide spaces between the lines and very wide margins surrounding the text. Luther would then fill in the empty space during lectures. Between the lines of text, definitions for words and grammatically important observations were made. In the wide margins, students would write commentary on the meaning of the passage under investigation. It is likely, though not proven, that in October 1517, Luther went again Johann Grünenberg, Wittenberg's early printer, and had him prepare a small number of copies of his *Disputation on the Power and Efficacy of Indulgences*. That disputation has come to be known as the *Ninety-Five Theses*. The theses were printed in Latin for use by his students and colleagues in Wittenberg and Luther intended to send a few copies to other universities and to his archbishop, Albrecht. They were not meant as a revolutionary treatise. That the *Ninety-Five Theses* became so famous was due to the printing press and to a German translation.

Very soon after Luther posted the *Disputation* for student discussion, and probably after the student debate over them, they were printed in Latin in Nuremberg, Strasbourg, and Basel. There are no copies of the possible edition from Wittenberg still in existence. We do have copies from the other three cities. Within weeks, the printed copies of the *Theses* were being posted off to universities across Europe. Erasmus, for example, sent them to his friend and the future chancellor of England, Thomas More. Clearly, Luther had struck a chord among the theologians. Frederick the Wise remarked, once he heard them, that the pope would not be happy with them. But, without the translation into German, they would not have had a wide public affect. The *Theses* were translated in Nuremberg by Caspar

Nützel, who was not a priest or theologian, but was a humanist minded city official. Over the next 12 months, according to Mark Edwards, there was over a 500 percent increase in German language propaganda much of it related to Martin Luther and the indulgence controversy. Of all the pamphlets, broadsheets, and books published in the 1520s, more than 20 percent of them were written by Martin Luther.[11] Without the printing press, Luther's ideas would have remained a debate among theologians alone.

THE ROAD FORWARD

This book is intended to be a helpful beginning guide to some of the more complex aspects of Luther's theology. It begins with a brief biography of Luther. The first thematic chapter begins where this chapter ends, the Indulgence Controversy, the *Ninety-Five Theses*, and Justification by Faith. Chapter 4 focuses on two central motifs in Luther's thought; the distinction between the Law and the Gospel on the one hand and the Theology of the Cross on the other. Chapter 5 looks one of Luther's most bitter theological debates, the argument with Desiderius Erasmus over the bondage or freedom of the human will as that will relates to salvation. Chapter 6 explores Luther's understanding of the Antichrist and the role of the Antichrist within the world. Luther ultimately came to see the papacy as embodying the Antichrist, this chapter will explain why he did so and how he came to that belief. Chapter 7 deals with Luther's view of political violence and resistance. May soldiers also be Christians? May a Christian resist an unlawful or tyrannical king or ruler? Both of those questions will be examined. Chapter 8 will discuss one of the two most controversial writings of Martin Luther: his diatribe against the peasants during the 1525 Peasants' War. Though he is undeniably harsh and vociferous, he was not the monster he has been portrayed as. Finally, Luther's other highly controversial writing will be discussed. In 1543, Luther published a tract against Jews titled, *Against the Jews and Their Lies*. It is disturbing to read, made all the more so because of the ways that the Third Reich used the treatise during World War II. How could Luther write such a document? That question may not be fully or completely answered in this chapter, but together we shall investigate some possibilities.

---

11 Edwards, *Printing, Propaganda, and Martin Luther*, 17.

CHAPTER 2

THE LIFE OF LUTHER

Biographies of Martin Luther abound. Great biographies of him, however, are a rarer find. For more than a century, the most thorough and complete biography of Luther was Julius Köstlin's two-volume 1875 *Martin Luther: Sein Leben und seine Schriften*.[1] Köstlin's biography was abridged and translated as a single volume in 1883 as *The Life of Martin Luther*.[2] Köstlin has now been succeeded but not entirely replaced by Martin Brecht's 1981–1987 three-volume *Martin Luther*, which was translated into English beginning in 1985.[3] Brecht's biography is both exhaustive and encyclopedic and will remain the authoritative examination of Luther's life for the foreseeable future. Numerous other (and shorter) biographies continue to pour out of popular and academic presses. The most important of these shorter biographies is Heiko Oberman's 1981 *Luther: Mensch*

---

1 Julius Köstlin, *Martin Luther: Sein Leben Und Seine Schriften*, 2 vols. (Elberfeld: Friderichs, 1875). In 1883, Köstlin expanded the biography significantly. Julius Köstlin, *Martin Luther: Sein Leben Und Seine Schriften*, 2 vols. (Elberfeld: Friderichs, 1883). It was republished in this edition again in 1889. In 1903, it was again significantly revised this time by Gustav Kawerau. Julius Köstlin and Gustav Kawerau, *Martin Luther: Sein Leben Und Seine Schriften*, 2 vols. (Berlin: Alexander Dunker, 1903). All three versions can be downloaded from Googlebooks. Köstlin remains extremely useful because of his exhaustive endnotes.

2 Köstlin, *Martin Luther: Sein Leben Und Seine Schriften*. This volume is also available on Googlebooks. It is a translation of the 1875 edition.

3 Martin Brecht, *Martin Luther*, 3 vols. (Stuttgart: Calwer, 1981–1987); Martin Brecht, *Martin Luther*, trans. James Schaaf, 3 vols. (Philadelphia: Fortress Press, 1985–1993).

zwischen Gott und Teufel, which was translated in 1989.[4] Among all Luther biographies, the sentimental favorite remains Roland Bainton's *Here I Stand*. Though it is certainly dated in both its approach and research (having been written in 1950) it remains unsurpassed as pure narrative.[5] Richard Marius's biography should be approached with caution and should not be read without also consulting Oberman's review of it.[6] A single chapter cannot hope to replicate what others have done in multivolume works. In this chapter, the main features and events of Luther's life will be highlighted. Those who wish to learn about any particular event in far greater detail should consult Brecht.

1483–1505

Martin Luther was born in Eisleben, in central Germany on 10 November 1483. His parents were Hans (d. 1530) and Margaritha (nee Ziegler; d. 1531) Lüder.[7] Hans and Margaritha had just recently moved to Eisleben from their family home in the small village of Möhra, just south of Eisenach. The move from Möhra to Eisleben was significant and a distance of over 80 miles. Hans was unable to inherit property in Möhra and so they moved to Eisleben in the hope of earning a better living. In Eisleben, Hans became a miner. According to Luther's mother, he was born late in the evening and the next morning (11 November) he was taken to the Church of Saints Peter and Paul where he was baptized and named in honor St. Martin of Tours as it was his feast day.

---

4 Heiko Augustinus Oberman, *Luther: Man between God and the Devil*, trans. Eileen Walliser-Schwarzbart (New Haven: Yale University Press, 1989); Heiko Augustinus Oberman, *Luther: Mensch Zwischen Gott Und Teufel* (Berlin: Severin und Siedler, 1982).

5 Roland Bainton, *Here I Stand: A Life of Martin Luther* (New York: Abingdon-Cokesbury Press, 1950).

6 Richard Marius, *Martin Luther: The Christian between God and Death* (Cambridge: Belknap Press of Harvard University Press, 1999); Heiko Augustinus Oberman, "Varieties of Protest: *Martin Luther: The Christian between God and Death*," *The New Republic*, 16 August 1999.

7 When exactly Luther changed the spelling of his name from Lüder to Luther is unclear. He was still using Lüder when he transferred to Wittenberg in 1508. See Karl Eduard Förstemann, *Album Academiae Vitebergensis: 1502–1602*, 3 vols. (Leipzig: C. Tauchnitz, 1841–1905), I: 28.

Not long after Luther was born, Hans moved the young family again. This time he moved them to Mansfeld. Though Mansfeld was a smaller town than Eisleben, it provided more opportunity for Hans. Luther's childhood was spent in Mansfeld and his father grew to relative prosperity as a copper miner in town. While Möhra was in Thuringia and thus ancestrally Luther was Thuringian, Mansfeld was part of Saxony and Luther always considered himself a native of Mansfeld and a Saxon.[8] Hans's prosperity allowed him to enroll his young son in the town's Latin school in 1491 when Martin was 7. The curriculum at the Mansfelt school would have been the classic *Trivium* of grammar, logic, and rhetoric. Later in life, Luther did not reflect back kindly on his teachers in Mansfelt and felt that they were unduly cruel to young boys struggling to learn a new language. In 1497 at 13, Hans moved Martin from the local Latin school to a boarding school in Magdeburg. He went to Wittenberg together with the son of a family friend in Mansfelt. Though the rationale is uncertain, Magdeburg was a large and important late medieval city and the educational opportunities it offered could not be attained in a small village such as Mansfelt. A year later, Hans moved the now 14-year-old again. This time, Martin was enrolled in the parish school of St. George in Eisenach. Eisenach might have been a compromise between the limited possibilities of Mansfelt and the expensive boarding school of Magdeburg. In Eisenach, too, Luther had many relatives. He boarded with the town's mayor, Heinrich Schalbe. In 1501, Luther completed his primary education and began life as a university student.

Hans Luther sacrificed a great deal in order to afford his son's education. Then, as today, education provided a means to social and economic advancement. Hans chose the University of Erfurt for Martin. Erfurt was a large city in the early sixteenth century. The university was a century old and its prominence outweighed its age. For the next 18 months, Luther studied the normal baccalaureate curriculum. In a sixteenth-century German university, a student had to complete the baccalaureate and master of arts degrees before advancing to specific graduate work in law, theology, or medicine. Hans Luther intended for Martin to become a lawyer. In the baccalaureate

---

8 For example, when he matriculated at Erfurt in 1501 as "Martinus ludher ex mansfelt" and when he transferred to Wittenberg in 1508 he is listed as "Fr. Marinus lüder de Mansfelt."

degree, students had to master the seven *artes liberales* (or liberal arts). The seven liberal arts were grammar, rhetoric, logic, arithmetic, geometry, music, and astronomy. Mastery of these subjects was demonstrated by examination, and Luther took his examinations in the fall of 1502.

For the next three years, he devoted himself to advanced work in philosophy, logic, mathematics, even music. In 1505, he graduated as second in his class for a Master of Arts degree. He was now prepared to enter the graduate program in law.

1505–1519

In November 1504, Luther turned 21. He was not, however, a frivolous and carefree youth. Earlier that year, or perhaps the year before, he badly injured himself with—of all things—a friend's sword. The idea of death and standing before God's final judgment terrified him. He refers to this fear of death and judgment as his *Anfechtungen*. *Anfechtung* or the plural *Anfechtungen* are important theological terms in the life of Luther and will remain untranslated in the rest of this book because there is no equivalent English word. For Luther, his times *Anfechtungen* were moments of intense fear, dread, and hopelessness. They were times when he felt as if he would die and knew that if he did die he would be cast into hell as punishment for his sins. These were not moments of temporary angst but of almost debilitating terror. Though he would eventually find grace and forgiveness in his life he never completely escaped being haunted by his *Anfechtungen* but that was still years into the future and in 1505 Luther was caught tightly in the grips of *Anfechtungen*. The year began with an outbreak of the plague in Erfurt that claimed the lives of some friends and teachers. Though people had learned a good deal about how to mitigate the chances of getting the plague since it first broke out in the 1350s, it was still largely a mysterious and terrifying disease that descended without warning. Seeing friends and colleagues die certainly heightened Luther's fear of death and judgment. After a brief visit to his parents in May and June of 1505, Luther began his journey back to Erfurt to continue his legal studies. When he was less than a half-day's journey from Erfurt he was caught out in the open during a violent thunderstorm. As I can personally attest, one need not be hit by lightening to feel its affects. The air crackles with electricity and the light flashes simultaneously with the explosion of thunder. One's hair prickles and if you are in a puddle your legs and feet vibrate with the electricity. In such a moment Luther screamed to the heavens, "Save me Saint Anne and I shall become a monk." The idea of becoming a monk was certainly not new to Luther and he had been contemplating it for some time most likely, but in this terrifying moment he made an irrevocable pledge. On 17 July 1505, Martin Luther knocked on the gatehouse door to the monastery of the Erfurt Augustinian Hermits.

In his first year as a monk, he devoted himself to the study of the Bible. Numerous new editions of the Bible were pouring off printing presses and Luther may have gained a copy for himself. After that initial year, it seems Luther began to study theology and Bible formally in the theology faculty at Erfurt. In 1508, he was transferred to Wittenberg to fill in as a philosophy teacher (his MA qualified him for that position). While in Wittenberg, he continued to study theology. After a brief journey to Rome and another stay in Erfurt, Luther finally returned to Wittenberg for good in 1512 (Figure 2.1). He transferred there to take a position on the Theology faculty and simultaneously finish a Doctor of Theology degree. He received that degree in October of 1512 and began teaching Bible in the fall of 1513.

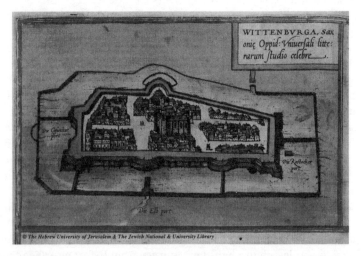

Figure 2.1 Wittenberg map from Braun and Hogenberg's *Civitates orbis terrarium*, 1572. Reprinted by permission of Historic Cities Research Project: http://historic-cities.huji.ac.il—The Hebrew University of Jerusalem, The National Library of Israel, Shapell Family Digitization Project.

Though we are not absolutely positive, it is relatively certain that Luther began his university lectures with a two-year cycle of lectures on the Psalms. Luther prepared for these lectures as he would prepare for all his lectures that followed. The first thing he did was commission a publication of the biblical text on large folio sheets. The biblical text was printed down the middle with wide margins on both sides and large spacing between each row of text. Between the rows of text, Luther wrote notes on grammatical issues and questions of translation or meaning for the words themselves (Figure 2.2). These

Figure 2.2 Image of Martin Luther's lecture notes for his 1515/1516 lectures on Romans. Taken from *Luthers Vorlesung über den Römerbrief 1515/1516*, edited by Johannes Ficker (Leipzig: Theodor Weicher, 1908), p. 163.

notes are called *glosses* and were typical in medieval university teaching. Luther gathered many of the grammatical and philological questions from a great compendium normally called the *Glossa Ordinaria*. In the wide side margins, Luther wrote and then dictated to his students the theological lessons that can be derived from the text. In these *scholia*, he also continued to use the medieval fourfold interpretation of scripture. When he completed the lectures on the Psalms, he moved on in 1515 to lecture on Romans. A number of important things happened during this series of lectures. First and foremost, Luther began to focus heavily on the work and thought of Paul. His understanding of grace and justification will be based in Paul, and in these lectures one can begin to see him grappling with the question of salvation. Second, while he continued to work with the *Glossa Ordinaria* he also began to find his own voice in lecture and was more willing here than he had been in the Psalms lectures to offer his own opinion. Third, the Romans lectures are the first lectures in which we see evidence of Luther's turn away from the Latin edition of the Bible to the original languages. In 1516, Desiderius Erasmus published his first edition of the New Testament in Greek. We do not know exactly when Luther got a copy, but it was soon after publication and you can see the effects of the Greek New Testament by his lectures on Romans 9. After that, the influence of Erasmus shows up on nearly every page.[9]

While Luther was lecturing to students, he was also expanding his other responsibilities. In Wittenberg, he was called on to preach and pastor at the city church. St. Marien is about two blocks from both the Wittenberg Castle complex where the university met and the Augustinian monastery where Luther lived. Within the life of the Augustinian monastery, Luther became in 1515 the district vicar for ten monasteries. This enormous administrative role occupied a great deal of his time and Martin Brecht argues that he approached the job with a constant eye toward caring for the souls of the brothers entrusted to his care.[10]

It was Luther's understanding of pastoral care—*Seelsorge*, or the care of souls—that also guided his response to indulgences and ultimately the writing of the *Ninety-Five Theses*. Indulgences originally

---

9 Martin Luther, *Luthers Vorlesung ÜBer Den RöMerbrief, 1515/1516* (Leipzig: Dieterich, 1908), xlvi and 83.

10 Brecht, *Martin Luther*, I: 156–7.

developed as a response to a pastoral care problem. In medieval theology, the stain and punishment of sin and the alleviation of God's judgment was dealt with through the sacrament of penance. The sacrament had three parts: *contritio, confessio*, and *satisfactio*. The first step—*contritio*, in English contrition—is the honest and remorseful repentance of the sinner for the sin committed. This remorseful repentance is then openly confessed to a priest who hears the "confession." Finally, the priest will give the sinner an act or group of acts of contrition to satisfy the justice of God. The way this developed is not difficult to understand. People often feel the need to do something constructive to make their forgiveness real. Acts of Contrition in contemporary popular imagination have been reduced to saying the Hail Mary or the Lord's Prayer, but in the medieval era they were often more difficult. Often times, people could not do everything required for "satisfaction." Without fulfilling the requirements of satisfaction, however, the sinner could not receive absolution for the sin committed. People who died without making the proper satisfaction fulfilled the requirements of satisfaction in purgatory. Out of the need to help those people who were in a sense "satisfaction deficient" the concept of indulgences arose. Indulgences could satisfy particular acts of contrition or could lower the number of days spent in purgatory. Acts of indulgence and satisfaction came in a many different forms—from pilgrimages to special holy sites, to prayers said before holy relics that reminded people of the saints who had lived more holy lives, to donations made to worthy church projects. Ultimately, indulgences could even be purchased for those who had already died and were currently in purgatory. Wittenberg's own duke and elector, Frederick the Wise, was one of the medieval era's greatest collectors of holy relics (Figure 2.3). In 1513, for example, his collection had 5,262 items that could satisfy nearly 42,000 years in purgatory. By 1518, the collection had grown to 18,970 items and the precise calculation of years in purgatory that could be satisfied had grown to 1,909,202 years and 270 days.[11]

---

11 Paul Kalkoff, *Ablass Und Reliquienverehrung in Der Schlosskirche Zu Wittenberg Unter Friedrich Dem Weisen* (Gotha: Friedrich Andreas Perthes, 1907), 64–6. See also, Carlos M. N. Eire, *War against the Idols: The Reformation of Worship from Erasmus to Calvin* (Cambridge: Cambridge University Press, 1989), 15–16.

Figure 2.3 Image of a Cross with 2 pieces from Christ's Crown of Thorns that was part of Frederick the Wise's reliquary at the Wittenberg Schloss Kirche from *Wittemberger Heiligthumsbuch* by Lucas Cranach the Elder, 1509; *Wittemberger Heiligsthumsbuch Facsimile-Reproduction*, edited by Georg Hirth, Munich, 1884.

Over time, Luther came to the belief that the power and efficacy of indulgences were illusionary. They provided false hope. In October of 1517, he proposed an academic debate for his students on the subject. The timing was not accidental. In the mid-twentieth century, there was a fierce debate over whether or not Luther nailed his *Ninety-Five Theses* to the door of the Castle Church in Wittenberg (Figure 2.4). Clearly, the iconic image of Luther standing at the door of the church ringing out a clarion call for revolt against papal abuse with each crack of the hammerhead is a myth. There is no evidence to support the idea that Luther intended a theological or ecclesiastic revolution in 1517. What is more likely is that Luther did indeed post the *Ninety-Five Theses* on the door of the church in order to alert his students of the upcoming classroom debate. The date of 31 October 1517 is also probably fairly close to accurate if not exact. The *Ninety-Five Theses* is shorthand for two documents actually.

Figure 2.4 Wittenberg Schloss, from *Wittemberger Heiligthumsbuch* by Lucas Cranach the Elder, 1509; *Wittemberger Heiligsthumsbuch Facsimile-Reproduction*, edited by Georg Hirth, Munich, 1884.

The first is a letter written by Luther to his bishop, Archbishop Albrecht of Mainz. In the letter, Luther alerts the archbishop to what Luther believed to be abusive tactics being used to sell indulgences in the archbishop's name. That Albrecht knew all about this did not occur to the somewhat naïve Luther. The second document was a copy of the debate theses Luther had written for his students. The *Theses* are one-sided and even a bit inflammatory on purpose. They are written to provoke debate. As disputation topics, one student or group of students would be assigned the responsibility of defending the theses and another group opposing them. The idea was that both sides would learn through the exercise of debate.

Thesis one sets the entire tone for the disputation: "When our Lord and Master Jesus Christ said, 'Penitentiam agite &c,' he intended that the entire life of believers should be one of repentance (penitentiam)." I have left the Latin in the sentence because it is important to understand exactly what is happening in the sentence. The quotation from Jesus comes from Matthew 4.17, in modern English translations that sentence reads, "From that time Jesus began to preach, saying, 'Repent, for the kingdom of heaven is at hand.'" This sentence was an often-used prooftext for the sacrament of penance. In the Latin Vulgate, the sentence reads, "Exinde cœpit Jesus prædicare et dicere: Poenitentiam agite: appropinquabit enim regnum coelorum."[12] What Luther noticed, however, when he began to read the New Testament in Greek was that *poenitentiam agite* was not a very good translation for the Greek word, *metanoiete*. What Luther discovered was that the text should not be read, "do penance," but "repent."

The practice of indulgences, even if they were once a pastoral response to people's truly felt need, had become a major funding avenue for bishoprics across Europe and also the Vatican. The market for them depended upon people's trust that they were effective. Their effectiveness was guaranteed by the pope. In a number of theses, Luther attacked the pope's ability to grant such a guarantee, his ability to forgive the sins of those already deceased, and urged the pope if he did have such power to use it to release all currently suffering in purgatory. Why, Luther asked, would one countenance the continued suffering of sinners if one could gracefully release them?

Within a very short amount of time, Luther's Latin *Theses* had been translated into German and set out for printing in the still new and revolutionary printing press. It is impossible to know now how many copies were published, but estimates run as high as 100,000 copies. Publishers do not print items solely out of generosity, and

---

12 *Biblia Sacra Veteris & Novi Testamenti* (Paris: Carloae Guillard, 1568), AAiiiir.

they clearly saw a market for the newly translated *Theses*. At first Albrecht of Mainz planned on ignoring Luther's letter. Later, he sent a copy on to the Vatican. Albrecht's letter and copy of the Luther's *Theses* arrived in Rome sometime in December. According to legend, Pope Leo X initially shared Albrecht's impulse to ignore the document. If he did, that impulse did not last long. Leo quickly turned to the official papal theologian (called the Master of the Sacred Palace), a Dominican monk named Sylvester Mazzolini. Called Prierias after his hometown of Prierio, Italy, he was a remarkably able theologian and a staunch defender of papal authority. Prierias immediately recognized the implied and direct threats to papal dignity in the *Theses* and responded with his own treatise, *Dialogue against the Theses of Martin Luther Concerning the Power of the Pope.*[13] It is important to notice how Prierias skillfully reframed the debate with Luther. Where Luther wrote on the power of indulgences, Prierias discussed the power of the pope. For Luther there was a distinction to be made between the two. For Prierias they were synonymous. In order to make this very clear to all, Prierias began the dialogue with four "Fundamental Principles." The first noted that the universal church was synonymous with the Roman Church and that the pope was the head of the church. Second, the pope is unable to err when discerning sacred doctrine. Third, whoever disagrees with either principle one or two is a heretic. Finally, in a direct confrontation to Luther, Prierias writes, "He who says regarding indulgences that the Roman Church cannot do what she in fact does is a heretic."[14] Prierias's *Dialogue* was then put together with a summons to appear in Rome within 60 days of its receipt. Luther received both documents on 7 August 1518. By that point, however, Rome had already decided that Luther had denied the power of indulgences and therefore was a heretic. A letter was sent to the papal legate in Germany telling him to have Luther arrested. Once arrested for heresy, he would be transferred to Rome, tried, and then burned at the stake. That this did not happen was the result of imperial politics, German nationalism, and Frederick the Wise's personal pride and ambition.

---

13 Silvester Mazzolini Prierias, *Ad Dialogum Silvestri Prieratis Magistri Palatii De Potestate Pape Responsio* (Leipzig: Lotther, 1518).
14 Ibid., fol. A2r.

What came to be called the "Luther Affair" was from almost its opening moments caught up in imperial politics of the highest order. Luther's prince, Frederick the Wise, was one of seven imperial electors. Set out in the Golden Bull of 1356, the position of emperor was elected rather than inherited. Seven men were designated as the officials charged with electing a new emperor. There were four temporal lords and three archbishops. They were the duke of Saxony (Frederick), the margrave (i.e., marques) of Brandenburg, the king of Bohemia, the count palatine of the Rhine, and the archbishops of Cologne, Trier, and Mainz. In late 1518, it became apparent that the aged emperor, Maximilian I, was dying. Frederick would now be called on to act as regent during an imperial interregnum and cast his vote for the next emperor. There were a number of candidates for the position. Among those with a direct interest in the position were Luther's archbishop and the pope. Albrecht of Mainz was the younger brother of the margrave of Brandenburg. Together they hoped to elect John of Brandenburg as the next emperor. The leading contender for the job was Charles Habsburg, Maximilian's 18-year-old grandson. Pope Leo X actively campaigned against Charles fearing that he would become a far too powerful potentate. Charles was already the king of Spain, king of Sicily, and the king of Naples having inherited those titles from his maternal grandparents, Ferdinand and Isabella. From his other grandfather he would soon inherit all of Maximilian's hereditary lands, including the Low Countries, the duchy of Burgundy and the archduchy of Austria. If he added the Holy Roman Empire to his long list of titles, he would completely surround the Papal Provinces. Thus, neither Leo X nor Albrecht of Mainz wished to do anything that might negatively dispose Frederick the Wise toward them. In fact, there is evidence to suggest that Leo X tried to persuade Frederick to assume the imperial title himself.

Frederick's increased clout within the empire allowed him to make a number of demands vis-à-vis the "Luther Affair." Two major impulses led Frederick to defend Luther. First was a nascent German nationalism. In the late medieval era, many Germans had felt put upon and abused by the papacy for quite a long time. There was even a legend in Germany that when their greatest emperor and hero, Frederick Barbarossa, met Pope Alexander III, Alexander forced Barbarossa to kiss his feet. As Barbarossa kissed one of the pope's feet, Alexander purportedly pressed his other foot down on the emperor's neck to humiliate him.[15] When Luther initially received the demand to turn himself into church officials in Rome, he asked for a hearing first in Germany. Frederick staunchly supported Luther's petition that he be heard and provided an opportunity to defend himself first in Germany before being forced to travel to Italy and be tried in Rome. Second, Luther's sudden rise to prominence helped put the University of Wittenberg on the map. Frederick founded the university in 1502. It was his greatest pride. Now, he had a certifiable academic star on the faculty. He was rather unwilling to simply hand over this star without being absolutely convinced that he had no other alternative.

Of course, a man as powerful as Frederick did have other alternatives. The first alternative was to have Luther discuss his newly publicized theological convictions at the upcoming Diet of Augsburg with the papal legate (or ambassador) to the diet, Thomas Cardinal Cajetan (Tommaso de Vio, 1469–1534). In many ways, an audience with Cajetan was more than Luther or Frederick could have ever hoped for. Cajetan was a reform-minded cardinal who recognized a number of abuses and who had worked to overcome them. He was also a scholar open to humanist insights. Frederick ensured that Luther was properly prepared for the meeting with Cajetan and also saw to it that Staupitz went with Luther as a mentor and, to be honest, guardian to make sure Luther did not waste this opportunity. In mid-October 1518, less than a year after the publication of the *Ninety-Five Theses*, Luther met with Cajetan in Augsburg. Luther arrived expecting a scholarly debate; Cajetan it seems expected to impress on the wayward monk the error of his ways and receive from him a full and complete revocation. Neither man got what he wanted. Luther began the meeting by prostrating himself before Cajetan—a good sign to Cajetan. Almost immediately, however, he announced that he had come to Augsburg to explain not to revoke. Cajetan, perhaps giving in to some frustration, actually engaged Luther in a bit of debate. While he was a reformist when it came to issues of moral lapse and social negligence, Cajetan was a staunch defender

---

15 That this event did not happen is less important than the fact that many sixteenth-century Germans believed that it did happen. See, Kurt Stadtwald, "Pope Alexander III's Humiliation of Emperor Frederick Barbarossa as an Episode in Sixteenth-Century German History," *Sixteenth Century Journal* 23/4 (1992): 755–68.

of papal authority and agreed with his Vatican counterpart that Luther's *Theses* were less about indulgences and more about papal authority.

Each having failed to convince the other of the correctness of his position and discretion winning the first day, they both retired with a pledge to return the next day. If anything, the next day went even worse. While discussing the authority of the pope to issue indulgences, Luther was backed into a corner and finally declared that the pope was in error and that he abused scripture by promulgating the idea of indulgences. Cajetan erupted and demanded that Luther immediately recant. It should be remembered that Luther was a monk under authority. He had pledged to be obedient to those over him when he first became a monk. From Cajetan's point of view, he had been more than accommodating toward the wayward monk but enough was enough. Now was the time to capitulate and obey. Instead, Luther refused. He was dismissed from the cardinal's presence and was not invited to return. Luther actually waited for a couple of days perhaps naïvely believing that the cardinal would change his mind. When Luther heard that the cardinal had no intention of changing his mind and was actually preparing to have Luther arrested, he fled the city quickly and returned home having failed to convince Cajetan of his position and having actually made his position even more radical by stating that the pope was in error.

Though Frederick was now in the uncomfortable position of having arranged for a meeting that failed completely, he also played for more time. Luther was garnishing considerable support for his position among the faculty at the University of Wittenberg, and other German universities were also declaring that his position had merit. In January 1519, the emperor died and the Luther Affair became a back-burner issue for all involved. The eyes of the Hohenzollern bothers (John of Brandenburg and Albrecht of Mainz), Charles Habsburg, the king of France, the king of England, and the pope now all turned toward Frederick, Elector of Saxony and regent of the empire. If Frederick ever considered assuming the imperial office himself, he does not seem to have done so for very long. Instead, he threw his support behind Maximilian's grandson. In June 1519, Charles Habsburg was elected Holy Roman Emperor. As part of his election, he pledged to support and defend a number of privileges that allowed lesser German princes wide autonomy within their realms. This *Election Capitulation* (*Wahlkapitulation*) also included a pledge that Luther would not be extradited to Rome without being given a hearing within the empire first.

While the eyes of much of the empire were focused on the election of a new emperor in Frankfurt, Luther and his colleagues on the faculty at Wittenberg accepted an opportunity to debate his theology at the University of Leipzig in July 1519. Because Luther had promised Frederick that he would refrain from further exacerbating his precarious position, Luther's senior colleague on the faculty Andreas Bodenstein von Karlstadt was charged with leading the Wittenberg contingent, aided by the school's newest professor, the 21-year-old Philip Melanchthon. A well-known, brilliant, and highly regarded professor of theology from the University of Ingolstadt, Johannes Eck represented the other side. After days of setting the parameters for the debate and hours of what all witnesses confirmed to be boring and dry debate, Eck finally succeeded in drawing Luther to the debate.

Eck was, to be fair to all involved, the better speaker and debater. He had a natural flair and an easy rapport with the audience that had gathered in the great hall of Leipzig's Duke George's castle. As he challenged Luther's position on indulgences, he also began to pull from Prierias's treatise and bind Luther to questions concerning the authority of the pope. Once he had established that groundwork, he got Luther to state that what truly mattered for a Christian was not his relationship to the pope but to Christ. He asserted that many Greeks had found salvation without aid of the bishop of Rome. Having won this capitulation from Luther, Eck used one of the most tried-and-true of debate techniques. He tied Luther's position to an already discredited position. In this case, he noted the similarities between what Luther was saying and what Jan Hus had proclaimed a century earlier. This was an incendiary charge in Leipzig because Hussites from nearby Bohemia had raided and attacked Leipzig within living memory. To be tied to not only a confirmed (and executed) heretic but also to a hated enemy was chilling, and Luther asked for a break to consider the accusation.

He took the break to visit the university library and read up on the events surrounding Hus's condemnation by the Council of Constance in 1414. There he discovered certain things in Hus with which he disagreed, but more importantly he found some aspects of Hus that were not only in line with his thinking but that came directly from St. Augustine. Fortified by his belief that Hus was not a heretic in all things he returned to the hall. Eck was unrelenting and finally got Luther to admit that if scripture agreed with Hus and disagreed with either the pope or the council then they were wrong and Hus was right. It was a tremendous assertion and Eck pounced on it almost immediately. Luther was a Saxon Hus. He held himself and his interpretation of scripture above either pope or council. What one sees in this debate is a hardening of the lines that ultimately separated Luther from Rome. What would one day come to be called the idea of *sola scriptura* (by scripture alone) breaks forth here clearly. For Luther, scripture has become the sole measure of all Christian theology. Where current practice diverges from scripture it must be abandoned.

The debate continued for a few more days, but the fireworks were largely over. Eck had won. He had gotten his opponent to side with a confirmed heretic. At some point either toward the end of the Leipzig Disputation, or more likely, as Luther's party was leaving the Disputation, they learned that Charles Habsburg had been elected emperor. This news would have lifted the spirits of the Wittenberg delegation despite Eck's victory. Charles was known to dislike the pope. He was a well-educated, humanist, reform-minded, former student of Desiderius Erasmus. In short, he was—as viewed in 1519—more than anyone in Wittenberg could have hoped for. Thus, Luther headed back to Wittenberg more committed to his belief that it was Christ's work that redeems the sinner not anything the sinner might do. He also returned to Wittenberg with the intention of learning more about Jan Hus. Meanwhile Eck, exultant in his triumph, headed for Rome where he would ultimately write the bull of excommunication against Luther.

As a result of Luther's further investigation into the works of Hus and Eck's prodding regarding the power of the pope, Luther began to have serious concerns regarding the papacy as an institution and wondered if the pope might actually be the Antichrist.[16]

THE 1520s

In 1520, Luther turned 37. The year itself would go down as one of the most significant in his life. He would write the three most important treatises of his career between July and November 1520.

---

16 *LW* 48: 111; *WABR* 2: 48–9.

The first treatise he wrote was the *Address to the Christian Nobility of the German Nation* (*An den Christlichen Adel deutscher Nation*). The title was chosen with great care. This is not an address to Christians in general. Neither is it a treatise to the nobility *as* nobles. It was dedicated to Emperor Charles V and other nobles quite specifically as *Christian nobles*. According to Luther, the papacy had barricaded itself behind a fortress of rhetoric in order to defend itself from any calls that it ought to reform its morally sinful and theologically corrupt ways. Because Rome refused to hear of any need for reform and because God has given the nobility a rank and station in society that provided nobles with a voice that could be heard and would be headed, Luther calls on the nobles to act in this emergency situation on behalf of their fellow Christians. As leaders in society and also as Christians, they could help their fellow congregants by calling for a church-wide council to amend the errors of the church while at the same time working within the churches within their realms to end abuses and begin preaching that adhered to the Word of God.

The reaction to *Address to the Christian Nobility* was almost as swift as the reaction to the *Ninety-Five Theses*. The idea that nobles and other leaders in society, such as city magistrates, could think and act as Christians might today seem commonplace, but was revolutionary when Luther wrote the treatise. Luther called these leaders "fellow-priests" who must act to bring down the walls of papal inaction. They must trumpet reform like Joshua at Jericho. Like Jericho, the walls of the Romanists stand against God and so they will fall if the Gospel is proclaimed. The idea of ordinary Christians— be they of great or small status—taking some role of authority within the medieval church was stunning. According to medieval tradition as told by the papacy, even an emperor's secular authority and power derived from the pope's authority on earth. Luther challenged all of this tradition. Against it, he stated that the situation was similar to a burning building in a city square. Yes, he admitted, the city's mayor as the head of the city's government ought to direct the efforts to fight the fire. But, he asked somewhat incredulously, what if the mayor was gone or refused to leave his own home during such a disaster? Should the rest of the city stand by and let a building burn because the mayor refused to do his job? Of course not. In such a situation, someone must step into the gap and lead the efforts to fight the fire. A fire, however, can only destroy a home or take a life—it could not touch immortality. A church that neglected to proclaim the

Gospel might never kill a man, but it could endanger his soul. Thus, if it is important to rush in to save his home or life, how much more important to aid his soul?

While Luther was calling on the nobility to reform the church, Pope Leo X was preparing his own treatise written to Luther himself and broadcast across Christendom. The bull *Exsurge Domine* declared that Luther's teachings were heretical and his works were banned. It required that he cease all writing and preaching and prayerfully reconsider his wayward opinions. He was given 60 days to recant his previous writings and return to the bosom of the church. It declared that if he should fail to do so, he would be considered a stubborn heretic and excommunicated. The bull left Rome on 10 June but did not reach Luther in Wittenberg until 10 October. Luther was never one to let a moment of rhetorical flourish pass him by and answered the papal bull with both speed and verve. He quickly penned a treatise against the bull that he titled, *Adverses execrabilem Antichristi bullam* (Against the Execrable Bull of the Antichrist) that was published on 1 December.[17] In order to make his points available to a wider audience, he also expanded the treatise and translated it into German a month later as *Widder die Bullen des Antichrists*.[18]

During time between the publication of *Address to the Christian Nobility* and the arrival of the papal bull threatening excommunication, Luther was anything but idle. During the summer and early fall months of 1520, he wrote the other two important treatises of 1520: *On the Babylonian Captivity of the Church* and *The Freedom of a Christian*. *On the Babylonian Captivity* (*De Captivitate Babylonica Ecclesiae*) (Figure 2.5) is perhaps the most theologically weighty of the three 1520 treatises. It is a thoroughgoing critique of the medieval system of the seven sacraments. In the treatise Luther denounces the tradition of withholding the communion cup from the laity. Traditionally in a Roman Mass, only the wafer—or the communion bread—was given to the laity. The cup was reserved for clergy alone. Luther could find no scriptural justification for this and so rejected it. Here we see him beginning to examine all church traditions by the plumb line of scripture. In scripture, Jesus said to the disciples, "Take eat, this is my body," but he also said, "Take drink, this is my blood poured out for you and for many for the forgiveness of sins." Luther

---

17 *WA* 6: 595–612.
18 *WA* 6: 614–29.

Won der Babylonischen gefengk
nuß der Kirchen/Doctor Martin Luthers.

Figure 2.5 Coverpage of the German Translation of the *Babylonian Captivity*; Martin Luther, *Von der Babylonischen Gefengknuß der Kirchen* (Strasbourg, 1520). Reprinted by permission of the Bayerische Staatsbibliothek, Munich.

understood both of these commands to be binding for Christian worship. You cannot follow only one-half of Christ's instructions. He also rejected the scholastic doctrine of Transubstantiation and the idea that the Mass was a recapitulation of Christ's sacrifice on the cross. It is unclear whether Luther meant this treatise for popular consumption because he did not translate it himself. Instead, a former supporter of Luther's published a translation. Thomas Murner was a well-known satirist who was also dedicated to ending a number of moral inadequacies within the church. While Murner initially believed that Luther was an ally in the fight against church failings, he changed his mind completely when he read *Babylonian Captivity*. Luther's assault on the sacramental system of the church went too far for Murner. He probably believed that broadcasting Luther's thought to a wider audience would convince others as it had him that Luther was not a reformer but a dangerous heretic. That hope failed when many more people read Luther's treatise in German and confounding Murner agreed with Luther.

The third treatise of 1520 is rightfully the most famous of the three and perhaps the most famous of all Luther's writings. Its tone and tenor are remarkably different from both of the earlier treatises. While in the first two treatises Luther comes across as a man full of righteous anger, here he presents himself with calm certitude. Pope Leo X has by now threatened him with execution, and yet Luther dedicates *On Christian Freedom* to Leo. It is too much to say that Luther was really naïve enough to believe that this treatise would convince Leo of his orthodoxy. On the other hand, Luther does come across in the treatise as one who does not wish to further fan the flames of discord. Here Luther is at his most persuasive.

The Freedom of a Christian begins with the paradox outlined by St. Paul in Romans. A Christian is perfectly free, servant of no one. A Christian is perfectly bound and subject to all. Luther here argues that as Christians people are free from the tyranny of the law and the fear of eternal damnation. Therefore, they are perfectly free. They are not subject before God to anyone. On the other hand, this freedom allows them to serve others not out of duty or fear but out of a genuine response to the freedom of the Gospel. They are called upon to serve their brothers and sisters. As Christ made clear in Gospels, our brothers and sisters, our neighbors, even include those who are our enemies.[19] Thus a Christian, freed from the tyranny of the law willingly places himself at the service of others and thus is a perfectly dutiful servant of all. A touchstone of Luther's theology from this point forward will be his use of and comfort with theological paradox.

The Freedom of a Christian was published in November 1520. On 10 December, Luther's 60-day grace period from the pope expired. Earlier in the month, Luther's writings had been burned in Cologne

---

19 See, for example, Matthew 5 and Luke 10.

and Mainz, and in Wittenberg there were rumors that his works were to be burned in Leipzig. Thus, it is probably not all that surprising that some of the university faculty and their students felt a fitting way to mark the end of Luther's grace period would be to have a bonfire themselves. Thus, around 10 a.m., Philip Melanchthon helped gather students and staff from the college near one of the town's gates. There they burned copies of canon law, scholastic theology, and Luther himself put a copy of *Exsurge Domine* onto the flames. Leo X did not let the 60-day grace period go by without notice either and on 3 January 1521, he issued Luther's bull of excommunication, *Decet Romanum Pontificem* (The Roman Pontiff declares). Luther was now, officially, a heretic. As such he was subject to immediate arrest and trial. That this did not happen was due to the influence and no small degree of political maneuvering on the part of Frederick the Wise.

Just a couple of weeks after the pope issued the bull of excommunication, the estates of the Holy Roman Empire began meeting in the Free Imperial City of Worms. At the diet, Frederick the Wise secured a hearing for Luther that would allow him to present his theology and to be judged to be in error or not. Luther received the emperor's summons to the diet in late March. He arrived in Worms, about 300 miles away, at the head of a triumphant procession on 16 April (Figure 2.6). After settling into his quarters, Luther was told that he would appear before the diet the next day at 4 p.m. He would answer the questions addressed to him and only those questions. Johann von der Eck, an aid to the archbishop of Trier, served as Luther's interrogator.[20] According to contemporary reports, Luther seems to have been a bit overwhelmed by the visage laid out before him when he entered the large reception hall in the bishop of Worms' residence which had been taken over for the meeting of the diet. Assembled before him were the estates of the empire: the emperor, greater and lesser nobles, and the chief prelates, bishops, cardinals, and abbots—all dressed in regal finery. That he was overwhelmed should surprise no one. Von der Eck began by identifying a large pile of books resting on a central table. He asked Luther if they were his and if he was finally willing to recant. An advisor to Frederick who was serving as an unofficial legal advisor to Luther bought him some time to think by asking that the titles of all the books be read aloud.

---

20 He should not be confused with Johannes Eck.

Figure 2.6 Cityscape of Worms showing the cathedral from Braun and Hogenberg's *Civitates orbis terrarium*, 1572. Reprinted by permission of Historic Cities Research Project: http://historic-cities.huji.ac.il—The Hebrew University of Jerusalem, The National Library of Israel, Shapell Family Digitization Project.

When the titles had finally been read aloud, Luther began to speak in a soft and shy voice. He acknowledged that the books were his. As to the question of revocation, he said that was a serious and weighty question that concerned the souls of men. He asked for a night of prayer to consider his answer. He was granted a day. Many pro-Luther accounts of that night show a resolute and unwavering man committed to the Gospel at all cost and in no fear of his life. Whether that was the case, we cannot know. It is almost certain, however, that Luther could not have escaped the reality of his situation and the similarity of his position to that of Jan Hus a century earlier. Though many assured him that he would come to no harm in Worms, as he walked into the hall on 18 April a part of him had to recognize that it was likely his last free movement. During the night he wrote out his response and memorized it. He first divided his works into three piles on the table. The first group were works of moral piety and Christian reflection that even his enemies found no quarrel with. It thus made no sense to recant anything written in that pile. In the second pile he placed his more controversial works on the abuses of the clergy and the papacy. This presented a more difficult conundrum. Even if he did overstate things here, he could not in good conscience recant them in totality because to do so would only encourage such abuses to continue. In the third pile he placed his most vitriolic pieces that often attacked individuals directly. These he acknowledged were not becoming to his station as a professor or a monk. He regretted their tone, but (and this was a significant but) he could not recant the theological truth expressed in them. Having begun in German, he restated his speech again in Latin. He comes across in the speech as both more conciliatory than he had been previously while essentially capitulating absolutely nothing. Von der Eck recognized this immediately. He demanded that Luther recant. He reminded Luther that universities and the church hierarchy had both judged his theology as heretical. He asked with profound sarcasm if Luther really believed that he was the only one who could correctly understand scripture. Luther then replied with four sentences that have become famous:

> Unless I am convinced by the testimony of the Scriptures or by clear reason (for I do not trust either in the pope or in councils alone, since it is well known that they have often erred and contradicted themselves), I am bound by the Scriptures I have quoted and my conscience is captive to the Word of God. I cannot and I will not retract anything, since it is neither safe nor right to go against conscience.
>
> I cannot do otherwise, here I stand, may God help me, Amen.[21]

---

21 *LW* 32: 112; *WA* 7: There has been some debate over whether or not Luther uttered the phrase "I cannot do otherwise, here I stand." The phrase does not appear in the report of the interview written by the papal nuncio Hieronymus Aleander that was published in Hagenau in 1521. It does appear in the version of the interview published in Wittenberg almost immediately after the diet. That version is often attributed to Georg Spalatin but it is also likely that Justus Jonas helped prepare it and Luther almost certainly contributed to it. See, Georg Spalatin, *Die Gancz Handlung Szo Mit Dem Hochgelerte D. Martino Luther Taglichen Die Weyl Er Auff Dem Keyserlichen Reychs Tag Tzu Wormbs . . .* (Wittenberg: n.p., 1521), B1v. See also, Adolf Wrede, ed., *Deutsche Reichstagsakten Unter Kaiser Karl V: Jüngere Reihe*, 4 vols. (Gotha: Friedrich Andreas Perthes, 1896), II: 582. Hereafter abbreviated *DR*. Whether or not he said those exact words, he certainly was provocative because though he thought Luther did an excellent job, Frederick the wise did note to Spalatin that he thought Luther was, "Much too bold for me." *DR*, II: 550, n. 1.

The next day, Charles V asked the estates of the empire to judge Luther a confirmed heretic. They demurred and hedged for more time to make a final decision. Charles did not need more time and read to the diet his own opinion of Luther. Here for the first time we glimpse the young Charles Habsburg stepping into his new role as Holy Roman Emperor. The speech was given in French and was almost certainly written by him without aid. The grandson of the late Catholic emperor and their Catholic Majesties of Spain pledged himself to the eradication of Luther's religious innovations and heresy.[22] Despite his own opinion of Luther, Charles V allowed Luther to leave Worms under the terms of the safe-conduct promise. Even after he had left Worms, Luther remained a topic of intense discussion and a month after Charles read his opinion to the diet, his views were made official in the Edict of Worms.[23] The Edict declared that Luther was a heretic and that any who aided him faced the same punishment as a heretic. He was to be handed over to imperial authorities for trial and almost certain execution. His books were to be burned.

Frederick the Wise recognized that the Edict was immanent and did two things to buy himself (and Luther) more time. First, he secured from Charles an exemption for himself and his agents from serving Luther with an arrest warrant.[24] Second, he decided to hide Luther from the world for the time being. On 26 April, Luther left Worms.[25] A week later while still on the road back to Wittenberg, a group of armed men descended upon Luther's small band. The men took Luther by force from the group. Once out of view of the party, Luther's captors untied him and allowed him to get on a horse. That night he rode into his own "Mighty Fortress," the Wartburg.

The stay in the Wartburg Fortress was uneasy but not unproductive. He was quartered in a small room above the fortress's chief who not

---

22 *DR*, II: 594–6, ET in Oscar Thulin, *A Life of Luther* (Philadelphia, 1966), 66.
23 *DR*, II: 643–61.
24 *DR*, II: 659–60, n. 1.
25 Charles honored the safe passage guarantee he had given Luther a month earlier. He would later regret that decision, though he likely had little choice. He was a very young man and very newly elected. He would have recognized that to arrest Luther meant angering Frederick. Frederick might not have been an emperor or even a king, but he was most certainly a man to be reckoned with.

only cared for Luther's well-being but also saw to it that he remained in the fortress safely secreted from the world. Luther grew ill from the overly rich food they ate in the castle compared with what he had eaten in the monastery. He disguised his appearance by growing out his hair and growing a beard in order to look more like a soldier than a monk (Figure 2.7). He refers to the time as his "kingdom of the birds," and his own Patmos. Patmos refers to the small barren island in the Aegean Sea that was used by the Romans for banishment. St. John is said to have written the book of Revelations there. Like St. John in Patmos, Luther used his time in the furtherance of scripture. Where John wrote, Luther would translate. In December 1521, he began to translate the New Testament from the Greek. It took him three months to translate it. Though there were already a few different German translations of the Bible, Luther's translation must be regarded as one of the greatest contributions not only to biblical

Figure 2.7 Luther disguised as Junker Jörg while hiding at the Wartburg Castle by Cranach the Elder, 1522. Taken from Julius Köstlin's *The Life of Luther* (New York: Longmans, 1905), p. 209.

translation but also to the wider German language. He adopted a style that was both literary and understandable. Its effect on German culture is similar to the effect of the King James Bible in English.

Luther's exile to the Wartburg Fortress ended at nearly the same moment that he finished the New Testament translation. He was recalled to Wittenberg because of a degrading and increasingly violent situation in Wittenberg. In late 1521, students and some faculty members from the university joined with a group of townspeople and began to disrupt church services. Their aim was not to prevent preaching to the people but the continuation of the medieval Mass that they now saw as sacrilegious. Students and townspeople—at the instigation of Andreas Bodenstein von Karlstadt—also burned religious images. Some students went so far as to destroy and deface religious statues and iconography in churches. On Christmas day, Karlstadt—who had served as the dean of the theology faculty at the university—defied the Elector and celebrated the Eucharist without wearing vestments and gave both the wine and the bread to the common people. Although students were ecstatic, a number of the leaders in town were less enthused. The next day, Karlstadt announced his intention to marry.[26] As if that were not enough to cause distress in the small university town, the next day three itinerant preachers arrived. The so-called Zwickau Prophets, because they were from the town of Zwickau, proclaimed the imminent return of Christ, declared that they did not need the Bible because God spoke directly to them, called on people to repent of their sins and prepare for the End Times, and spoke out against infant baptism. The Prophets added fuel to an already incendiary situation. On 1 February students and townspeople rioted and burned, defaced, and destroyed religious iconography and beat up some monks. When parents began to discover what was happening in the town, they immediately recalled their sons. The university teetered on closing. The town teetered on total anarchy. On 20 February, without even consulting the Elector, the city council wrote to Luther and begged him to return. He received the letter a little more than a week later and immediately prepared to leave. On the evening before he left, he received a letter from the Elector telling him to remain in the

---

26 The fact that Karlstadt (a priest) was going to marry anyone was controversial. That she was 15 and more than 20 years his junior was also a point of some contention.

Wartburg. Frederick had learned of the council's letter and wished for Luther to remain hidden until after an upcoming imperial diet. Despite the Elector's request, Luther left the Wartburg. He wrote Frederick and explained that he had to return to Wittenberg to calm the discord and preserve the preaching of the Gospel. He felt that he had no other choice. He also realized that Frederick could do little to protect him should he fall into the hands of imperial forces. He told Frederick that, "I do not intend to ask your Grace's protection."[27] Leaving the Wartburg was perhaps the most perilous decision of his life. Without Frederick's protection he faced arrest, trial, and execution.

He remained in disguise throughout his journey from Eisenach (the small town below the Wartburg Fortress) to Wittenberg.[28] At one stop along the way dinner companions thought he might be Luther while others said that he was surely the knight Ulrich von Hutten. Luther joked that perhaps he was the mystical figure Prester John but left without giving them any name.[29] Luther arrived safely in Wittenberg on 6 March 1522; he would not leave the city except for short journeys on official business for the rest of his life. He immediately turned his attention to calming the discord in the town. Over eight days he preached eight separate sermons on the course of reform and the need for charity with each other. In the sermons, Luther argued that the pro-reform students and faculty members had been most uncharitable with their fellow Christians. They had destroyed images, broken with church tradition regarding marriage and the Mass, and behaved poorly throughout. Luther, it should be said, did not disagree with the intentions of the reformers. However, no matter that how well intentioned the reform, if it is forced upon someone's conscience it is not a reform at all but a new law. Luther's disagreement with Karlstadt had little to do with the types of reform, or even really the speed of implementation. Where Luther found fault was in how the reforms were implemented and why. Luther himself had argued for communion to the laity in both kinds, he was really indifferent about images, and was open to clerical marriage. Karlstadt's reforms were not the problem. For Luther, all these

27 *WABR* 2: 455; compare *LW* 48: 390.
28 It is about 150 miles between the towns.
29 Johannes Kessler, *Sabbata: Mit Klieineren Schriften Und Briefen* (St. Gallen: Fehr'sche Buchhandlung, 1902), 79.

reforms were opportunities for the congregation—not commands. However, by forcing them upon people they turned the Gospel into a new Law. This had to be resisted because if the Gospel is transformed from a gift to a requirement, then the proclamation of the church is destroyed:

> Love, therefore, demands that you have compassion on the weak . . . if I had seen priests holding mass, I would have preached to them and admonished them. Had they heeded my admonition, I would have won them; if not, I would nevertheless not have torn them from it by the hair or employed any force, but simply allowed the Word to act and prayed for them . . . In short, I will preach it, teach it, write it, but I will constrain no man by force, for faith must come freely without compulsion. Take myself as an example. I opposed indulgences and all the papists, but never with force. I simply taught, preached, and wrote God's Word; otherwise I did nothing. And while I slept, or drank Wittenberg beer with my friends Philip and Amsdorf, the Word so greatly weakened the papacy that no prince or emperor ever inflicted such losses upon it. I did nothing; the Word did it all.[30]

Finally, Luther argued that rebellion, discord, and property damage were never appropriate reactions regardless of the situation. The discord in Wittenberg quieted. The Prophets left town after a brief discussion with Luther. Karlstadt soon resigned from the university, took on the new name "Brother Andy," and assumed the pastorate in Orlamünde. He would stay there until his activities there so alarmed Frederick that he was expelled from Saxony entirely.

Over the next year and a half, Luther would be surrounded by relative calm in Wittenberg. He settled into teaching, began working on treatises that focused on the Christian life, and organized the new life of the university. Imperial officials seeking to arrest him never materialized. But even in this tranquility, storm clouds continued to form on the near horizon.

In 1520, Thomas Müntzer, who for a time resided in Wittenberg and was known there, became a pastor in Zwickau and certainly helped form the Prophets who left there and disturbed Wittenberg. Before the Prophets had even left Zwickau however, Müntzer had

---

30 *LW* 51: 77, translation altered. Compare, *WA* 10^III: 19.

been expelled from the city. For a year he then traveled in and around Prague. In 1524, he secured a position as the pastor in Alstedt (about 60 miles southeast of Wittenberg). In Alstedt, Müntzer began to reform the practices of the church, including the banning of infant baptism and the burning down of the chapel dedicated to the Virgin Mary. These actions gained Müntzer a summons to appear before the elector's court. In July 1524, he appeared before Frederick's brother (John the Constant) and nephew (John Frederick) where he tried to enlist their help in purifying the church and world.[31] The ungodly, he told them, have no right to live. They must become God's avengers. They must appoint him to be (as Daniel was to Nebuchadnezzar) their spiritual guide in this holy campaign. They demurred and Müntzer was expelled from his post. Thus repelled by the princes, Müntzer over the next year gathered around him an army of disaffected peasants and serfs who would follow him in this campaign. The full history of the Peasants' War will be discussed in Chapter 8, but here it is important to note just a few things. First, Luther worked tirelessly during the initial phases of the War to bring it to a peaceful and just conclusion. Second, when the violence looked as though it was spiraling out of control he wrote a passionate and vitriolic denunciation of the peasants. Finally, he was horrified by carnage at the Battle of Frankenhausen and the wholesale slaughter of the peasant forces there.

Even if the events of the Peasants' War and Luther's response to it had never happened, 1525 would have been one of the most important years in his life both personally and theologically. In November 1524, nine escaped nuns arrived in Wittenberg where they renounced their vows to monasticism and sought a new—and hopefully married— lives. They had come to the Reformation and rejected monastic vows because of Luther, and he felt responsible for their fates. Beginning in early 1525, he sought suitable suitors for them. By June, one remained; the daughter of a lesser noble, Katherina von Bora (1499–1552). At first, Luther considered the idea of asking Katherina to marry him a ridiculous idea. His father did not. His father advised him to marry her, and this seems to have had a major effect on Luther's view of Katherina. It must be said that he was not in 1525 a

---

31 He preached to John and John Frederick and because they were considered princes within the empire, this sermon is often called Müntzer's Princes Sermon.

romantic in general or as it specifically regarded Katherina. They wed, according to him, as much to enrage the pope as to confirm their love.[32] Over time, however, Luther grew to see in Katherina not merely a companion for life's journey but the deep love of his life. Together they had six children, four of whom lived into adulthood.[33] Their oldest child, Hans, was born in 1526.

Theologically, 1525 was important because of his intense debate with Desiderius Erasmus concerning the power and efficacy of the human will. Erasmus was the sixteenth-century's most renowned scholar. As we noted earlier, his influence on Luther should not be diminished. Early on in Luther's debates with Rome, Erasmus could be counted among Luther's supporters. Over time, however, he became more and more critical. Finally, by 1525, he engaged Luther directly. The full context of their debates over the will are discussed in Chapter 5. Here we must note that the break between Erasmus and Luther severed ties that Luther had hoped might aid the cause of reformation. The cost of remaining collegial, however, was too high. Luther would not jeopardize theological fidelity for political opportunity.

In 1526, the imperial diet met at Speyer and because of larger issues within the empire the members of the diet decided to temporarily suspend the 1520 Edict of Worms. Now each jurisdiction within the empire had the ability to decide how far and to what extent the Edict of Worms would be enforced until a church-wide council could be called to deal with all of the issues concerning Luther and religion within the empire.[34] Many Lutheran-leaning estates used

---

32 *WABR* 3: 482.
33 Two daughters died in childhood. The first died at just 8 months old, Katherina blamed a bout with the plague during her pregnancy with permanently weakening the baby. Even more tragic was the death of Magdalena in 1542. Luther's grief at her death was nearly inconsolable.
34 *Neue und Vollständigere Sammlung der Reichs-Abschiede* (Frankfurt: Kock, 1747), II: 274 §4. ET in B. J. Kidd, ed., *Documents Illustrative of the Continental Reformation* (Oxford: Clarendon Press, 1911), 185: "Thereupon have we, the Electors, Princes, Estates of the Empire, and ambassadors of the same, now here at this present Diet, unanimously agreed and resolved, while awaiting the sitting of the Council or a national Assembly . . . with our subjects, on the matters which the Edict published by His Imperial Majesty at the Diet held at Worms may concern, each one so to live, govern, and carry himself as he hopes and trusts to answer it to God and His Imperial Majesty."

Speyer to begin the implementation of reforms.[35] As part of this project, Luther and the leadership in Wittenberg began a series of church visitations. These visitations assessed the degree to which reforming principles were being received and understood. As a result of these visitations, Luther realized that more had to be done to explain Reformation theology to regular people. He wrote two catechisms for use within churches. The Small Catechism was designed for use in families and for parish clergy to help educate laity that were illiterate. The entries are short enough that they can be memorized. The Large Catechism was designed for educated pastors to explain themes in greater depth.

The 1520s began with Luther's life and the future of reform in great jeopardy and nearly ended on a similar note. In March 1529, another imperial diet met in Speyer. Between 1526 and 1529, while Lutherans were organizing their new churches, Catholics were organizing their opposition to Luther. When in the middle of the month the diet turned its attention to religious innovation within the empire, the estates quickly repealed the actions of 1526. The Edict of Worms was reinstated. In response to the repeal of 1526, the reinstatement of Worms, and because of the way in which both were handled by the diet, six rulers and fourteen imperial cities issued a formal protest (*Protestatio*) to Charles V's brother Ferdinand who was chairing the diet.[36] The formal protest gave Protestants their name and bought

---

35 There has been a good bit of controversy regarding this point. Leopold von Ranke asserted that the Recess gave legal authority for reform (see, *German History in the Age of the Reformation*, Bk. IV, ch. 2), others (most notably, W. Friedensburg, "Die Reformation und der Speierer Reichstag von 1526, *Lutherjahrbuch* 8 (1926): 195) have disagreed with him, seeing the Recess as a delaying tactic only. Though Friedensburg may be right on the details, Ranke is clearly correct in the way in which the *Recess* was used practically: the princes and estates used the *Recess* to further the cause of reform.

36 *Deutsche Reichstagsakten* VII/2: 1260–5. See also Johannes Kühn, *Die Geschichte des Speyrer Reichstags, 1529* (Leipzig: Schriften des Vereins für Reformationsgeschichte, 1929); Eike Wolgast, "Protestation of Speyer," in *Oxford Encyclopedia of the Reformation* (New York: Oxford University Press, 1996), 4: 103–5. The "Protestants" included Elector John the Constant of Saxony, Margrave George of Brandenburg-Ansbach, the dukes Ernst and Franz of Braunschweig-Lüneburg, Landgrave Philipp of Hesse, Prince Wolfgang of Anhalt, and the cities of Strasbourg, Nuremberg, Ulm, Constance, Lindau, Memmingen, Kempten, Nördlingen, Heilbronn, Reutlingen, Isny, St. Gall, Weissenburg, and Windsheim.

Luther's allies some time to organize themselves. The following year they would present their theology—now matured by a decade of refinement directly to the emperor.

THE 1530s

The events at the Diet of Speyer in 1529 meant that little could actually be accomplished in the empire politically. This political stagnation loomed large as the emperor and leading nobles tried to organize the empire to resist further incursions into Europe by the Ottoman Turks. In October 1529, Suleiman attacked Vienna. The Siege of Vienna shook many in Europe to their core. Charles V had to respond and immediately set to preparing the empire to defend itself against another attack. In the sixteenth century, religious diversity and disagreement seemed to exacerbate the Turkish threat. Unity had to be found. To that end, the emperor wrote to the Protestant estates and had them formulate a brief summary of their theological convictions. Luther could not travel to Augsburg because it is outside of Saxony. He traveled with the Protestant delegation up to the border and then stopped. He did help prepare the short defense of evangelical reforms. However, when the delegation arrived in Augsburg, it quickly became apparent that a short and simple defense of evangelical reforms was insufficient. Philip Melanchthon then wrote a more formal and lengthy explanation of Protestant faith. The resultant *Augsburg Confession* is one of the finest and clearest defenses of Protestant thought written in the sixteenth century. Melanchthon was also deeply aware of the broader issues within the empire and so the *Confession* goes to great lengths to stress the essential unity of the church (Articles 7 and 8) and the duty of Christians to serve the "public order and secular government" (Article 16).[37] Luther was frustrated at being removed from the primary writing of the document but was kept abreast of the situation. He would later write a defense of the *Augsburg Confession*. Those who posit some disagreement between Luther and the *Confession* gloss over Luther's own words to the contrary.

---

37 For a full discussion of the events that led up to the Augsburg *Confession* see Wilhelm Maurer, *Historical Commentary on the Augsburg Confession*, translated by H. George Anderson (Philadelphia: Fortress Press, 1986).

After the Diet of Augsburg, Protestant estates within the empire continued to feel threatened by the emperor. They formed a defensive alliance called the Schmalkaldic League. Luther wrote a treatise in support of the League and its agenda of supporting the empire against external threats while internally supporting the idea that religious diversity was acceptable. Luther's *Warning to His Dear German Nation* was widely published in 1530 and then again in the late 1540s when a war broke out between the emperor and the League.

In 1535, Luther began what would become his longest and most in-depth study of the Bible. From 1535 until just before his death a decade later, Luther lectured on Genesis. Throughout the lectures, one can now see the influence of core doctrines of the Reformation—such as justification by faith—helping to frame biblical exegesis. For example, the drunkenness of Noah was often excused in the medieval era. Not so with Luther. Instead he used the event to show that even great Patriarchs like Noah could sin and fall short and therefore were justified as much as any other person because of grace not works.

Throughout this time he was also the dean of the theological faculty in Wittenberg and dedicated himself to establishing an evangelical approach to theological education. He also continued to negotiate with Vatican officials about the convening of a church-wide council to consider the reforms that he had by now advocated for more than 20 years. These later years also saw some of his most angry and vitriolic works. His venomous work *On the Jews and Their Lies* is only the most well known. These works are discussed more fully in Chapter 9.

LUTHER'S DEATH

Luther had suffered from angina since the late 1520s. Angina is a condition in which the arteries of the heart are clogged, causing a constriction of blood. The pain can be intense, but it is not the same thing as a heart attack in which blood is completely cut off from a part of the heart that then dies. On 1 February 1546, while walking to Eisleben to oversee negotiations regarding economic strife in the town, Luther suffered the first of multiple heart attacks he would endure over his last two weeks. He records that he was overcome with sweat and passed out. He also records severe pain radiating down his left arm, tightness in his chest, and shortness of breath.[38] As we know

---

38 *WABR* 11: 277–8; *LW* 50: 292; Letter to Melanchthon 1 February 1546.

now, these are the telltale signs of a heart attack. A week later, he had a similar episode. Finally on 17 February, after eating dinner he suffered another heart attack. He was taken to a bed and given what people then believed was a mild sedative.[39] Later that night he had a final heart attack. His assistant Justus Jonas, aware that his death would be a moment of glee for his enemies and tragedy for his followers asked him, "Reverend Father, are you ready to die trusting in your Lord Jesus Christ and to confess the doctrine which you have taught in his name?" Luther answered, "Yes." He then died. He did not receive Last Rights nor give a final confession of his sins. Instead, he gave a final testament to his faith. His body was returned to Wittenberg. On 22 February, his community gathered to mourn his loss and proclaim the mystery of their faith—that he who was dead now rested with his Savior. Luther's old friend and the pastor of the city church, Johannes Bugenhagen, officiated at the funeral and Melanchthon gave the eulogy. He was buried beneath the pulpit in the Castle Church. For a man dedicated to proclaiming the Word of God, a more fitting place to rest could not have been found.

---

39 The records indicate that the Countess Anna of Mansfeld gave him grated unicorn horn. It was most likely the grated horn of a Narwhal whale, which does have a single horn.

PART II

LUTHER'S THEOLOGY FOR THE PERPLEXED

CHAPTER 3

JUSTIFICATION BY FAITH

In 1522, Martin Luther published his first edition of the New Testament translated into German. The translation was an instant publishing success. It was also controversial. One of the most controversial aspects of the work was a decision Luther made when he tried to put Romans 3.28 into German (Figure 3.1). When he got to that verse he added a word that does not appear in the Greek. The King James Version translates the sentence, "Therefore we conclude that a man is justified by faith without the deeds of the law." In Luther's German version, he added the word *allein* so that if we did the same thing in English that he did in German the sentence would read, "Therefore we conclude that a man is justified through faith alone without the deeds of the law."[1] The insertion of "alone," in the sentence caused an almost instantaneous stir. An adversary in the German city of Leipzig mocked him for trying to somehow perfect the Apostle Paul. Luther seems to have ignored the controversy but when he again turned to a major translation project in 1530, he returned the infamous *allein* and defended his insertion. His first defense was that the *allein* was necessary in order to make the

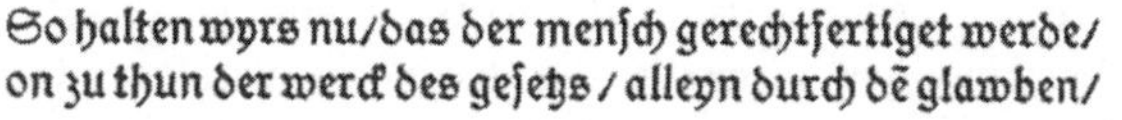

Ꙫo halten wprs nu/bas ber menſch gerechtfertiget werbe/
on ʒu thun ber werck bes geſeʒs / alleyn burch bẽ glawben/

Figure 3.1 Romans 3.28 containing the famous "alone" added to the text, "through faith alone [alleyn durch dẽ glawben]" from the 1522 Luther translation of the Bible; *Das Newe Testament Deützsch*, facsimile edition edited by Gustav Kawerau, Berlin, 1918.

---

1 Luther's actual German text: "So halten wyrs nu, das der mensch gerechtfertiget werde, on zu thun der werck des gesetzs, alleyn durch den glawben."

sentence read correctly in German as German. A translator, he noted, sometimes has to take license with the literal words in order to actually be faithful to the new language that the text is being translated into. After he clarified other places where it would not make sense to translate word-for-word, he moves on to the far more important explanation for adding *allein*, that it was theologically necessary. Luther writes, "Now I was not relying on and following the nature of the languages alone, however, when, in Romans 3[.28] I inserted the word *solum* (alone). Actually the text itself and the meaning of St. Paul urgently require and demand it. For in that very passage he is dealing with the main point of Christian doctrine, namely, that we are justified by faith in Christ without any works of the law. And Paul cuts away all works so completely, as even to say that the works of the law—though it is God's law and word—do not help us for justification . . . When all works are so completely cut away—and that must mean that faith alone justifies—whoever would speak plainly and clearly about this cutting away of works will have to say, 'Faith alone justifies us, and not works.' The matter itself, as well as the nature of the language, demands it."[2] For Luther justification by faith was the central and defining doctrine in his theology.

Luther arrived at his understanding of justification by faith gradually during the 1510s. His perspective on justification was markedly different from the theological understanding he had been taught in school and experienced in monastic life. In school and in the monastery, Luther was exposed to and deeply influenced by the theology of Gabriel Biel (1420–1495). Gabriel Biel was one of the greatest theologians of his age and was one of the founders of the University of Tübingen. One of Luther's professors in Erfurt had been a junior colleague of Biel's before moving to the University of Erfurt. Perhaps just as much as Luther, Biel believed that salvation was due to God's overwhelming grace. He differed from Luther, however, in how he understood that grace. According to Biel, God asks each man and woman to strive for holiness by "that which is within us to do." The phrase Biel used was *facere quod in se est*. Perhaps not everyone can, in fact, live a life of perfect sanctity like a saint, but we can each strive to do the best that we can. Then, according to Biel, God will look with grace on that striving. God will see that one is seeking to live a more holy life and doing the best that one can. When God sees this,

---

2 Luther, "Open Letter on Translating" (1530); *LW* 35: 195.

God will, in complete graciousness, give one the gift of making that striving a habit: *facienti quod in se est Deus non denegat gratiam* (God will not deny his grace to anyone who does what lies within him). When one's striving becomes a habit, God will look at one's new holy life and actions as meritorious. This merit will help us advance toward life's true end and goal—salvation. Biel understood his theology to be a completely gracious outlook on salvation. From Biel's perspective, one did not have to "be perfect as the Father in heaven is perfect," in order to be saved. One didn't even need to be as perfect as some of the saints. All that one did have to do was try to be as good a person as one could be. To those who did not strive, did not even try however, the same God who looks on the one who tries with grace will now look upon the one who did not in terrifying judgment. The *iustitia dei*—the justice of God—demands such a judgment.

The problem, both personally and theologically, for Luther with this system was one of surety. How could one be sure that one had done enough to merit God's gift of making one's striving a habit? How could one be sure that instead of a gift of grace one might very well receive the condemnation of judgment? He was haunted by the image of Christ as the judge of the world. In a popular image of the Last Judgment, Christ is seated in judgment with a sword in one hand and a lily in the other (Figure 3.2). Who knew, from Luther's perspective, whether one would receive the sword or the lily? Over the years, Luther had devoted himself to striving for justification before God as judge. When he visited Rome on behalf of his monastery in 1510/1511, he crawled on his knees up the stairs of the *Scala Sancta*. These are supposedly the stairs from Pontius Pilate's palace in Jerusalem that were moved to Rome in the fourth century. Popular piety said that these were the very stairs Jesus climbed before being condemned by Pilate to die on the cross. Thus, climbing the stairs on one's knees and reciting the Lord's Prayer was an act of deep devotion and would earn benefits of penance for oneself or a loved one. Luther climbed the stairs on behalf of his grandparents. He had hoped such an enterprise would prove deeply pious. Instead he arrived at the top of the stairs and felt nothing. People were hurrying him up in order to make room for more crowds of people. There was nothing reverent about the event. He remarked much later that he arrived in Rome with onions and left with garlic.[3] What

---

3 *WA* 47: 392.

Albrecht DÜRER   Small Passion -- LAST JUDGEMENT

Figure 3.2 Image of the Last Judgment with Lily and Sword at Christ's head; Albrecht Dürer, *Passio Christi ab Alberto Durer*, 1511. Taken from *The Work of Dürer: Reproduced in over Four Hundred Illustrations* (New York: Brentano's, 1907), p. 247.

he meant was that he went to Rome with some uncertainty and left with even more.

As we discussed in Chapter 2, Luther was also plagued by intense moments of *Anfechtungen* that overwhelmed him with a sense of his own condemnation before God. In an attempt to overcome these moments of deep anxiety, Luther dedicated himself to the search for salvation and a gracious God within the rigors of monastic life itself. Later in life, he wrote about his time in the monastery:

> When I was a monk, I made great effort to live according to the requirements of the monastic rule. I made a practice of confessing and reciting all my sins, but always with prior contrition; I went to confession frequently, and I performed the assigned penances faithfully. Nevertheless, my conscience could never achieve certainty but was always in doubt and said: "You could have done this correctly. You were not contrite enough. You omitted this in your confession."[4]

For Luther, justification before the terrifying visage of Christ in judgment remained illusive. He sought out his mentor and spiritual advisor so often that Staupitz finally lost patience with the young man and told Luther, "Look here," he said "if you expect Christ to forgive you, come in with something to forgive—parricide, blasphemy, adultery—instead of all these peccadilloes."[5]

Luther would continue to be haunted by Christ as the terrible judge for years. He also, most likely, continued to pester his confessor with peccadilloes. However, during the mid-1510s, Luther's thought regarding justification and his own personal salvation begins to go through a radical and complete change. In 1515, he began to lecture at the University of Wittenberg on the book of Romans. Luther's theology from that point forward will have a decidedly Pauline focus. The key passage in Romans for Luther's later understanding of justification is 1.17. There Paul writes, "For in it [the Gospel] the righteousness of God is revealed through faith for faith; as it is written, 'The one who is righteous will live by faith.'" When Luther lectured on this text in 1515, we can already begin to see the contours of his later thought. After he defined some of the terms in the sentence, he goes on to explain what the text means theologically. There he says,

> Only in the Gospel is the righteousness of God (*iustitia dei*) revealed (that is, who is and becomes righteous before God and how this takes place) by faith alone (*per solam fidem*), by which

---

4 Luther, *Lectures on Galatians*, LW 27: 13.
5 Bainton, *Here I Stand*, 54.

the Word of God is believed, as it is written in the last chapter of Mark (16:16): "He who believes and is baptized will be saved; but he who does not believe will be condemned." For the righteousness of God is the cause of salvation. And here again, by the righteousness of God we must not understand the righteousness by which He is righteous in Himself but the righteousness by which we are made righteous by God.[6]

This quote is important because it highlights two significant movements beyond Gabriel Biel in Luther's thought. First and foremost, Luther has begun to reframe his understanding of the righteousness of God. The righteousness of God is no longer viewed solely as a threat of judgment; it is, instead, a gift that to the sinner that is the "cause of salvation." Luther gained this new-found perspective from his reading of St. Augustine. In fact, Luther quotes Augustine on this very point in the next sentence. The second important trend we find established in this quote is Luther's commitment that it is faith alone which justifies. Luther will not use the phrase "sola fide" terribly often throughout his life, but it is a core idea within his thought and its presence here is important. Years later, he would remember his theological journey to an understanding of justification by faith alone in somewhat romantic terms but the kernel of his remembrance is certainly genuine:

At last, by the mercy of God, meditating day and night, I gave heed to the context of the words, namely, "In it the righteousness of God is revealed, as it is written, 'He who through faith is righteous shall live.'" *There I began to understand that the righteousness of God is that by which the righteous lives by a gift of God, namely by faith.* And this is the meaning: the righteousness of God is revealed by the Gospel, namely, the passive righteousness with which merciful God justifies us by faith, as it is written, "He who through faith is righteous shall live." Here I felt that I was altogether born again and had entered paradise itself through open gates. There a totally other face of the scripture showed itself to me. Thereupon I ran through the Scriptures from memory. I also found in other terms an analogy as, the work of God, that is, *what God does in us*, with which he makes us strong, the wisdom of

---

6 Luther, *Lectures on Romans* (1515/1516), *LW* 25: 151; *WA* 56: 171–2.

God, with which he makes us wise, the strength of God, the salvation of God, the glory of God.[7]

Luther here summarizes what has traditionally been called the "Reformation Breakthrough." It is best, however, to think of this less as a sudden earth-shattering bolt of revelation despite Luther's reminiscences in 1545. It is apparent in reading the Romans lectures that as he read and prepared to teach Paul, he was constantly struggling with a new understanding of justification. As those lectures evolved, so did his thinking. For example, in his lecture on Romans 4, he first focuses on the idea that righteousness is imputed (or granted) to people solely as a gift from God and not because of anything that one does. Or, just as importantly, in Romans 5 he first discusses the idea that because people are justified by faith separate from works of righteousness they are simultaneously saints (because God has declared them justified) and sinners. Let us now turn to discuss these three points in more detail.

SOLA FIDE—LUTHER'S CONCEPT OF FAITH

If, as Luther's translation of Romans 3 makes clear, we are saved by "faith alone," then it is imperative that one understand what Luther actually meant when he used the word faith. Luther was not, like his younger colleague Melanchthon or onetime follower John Calvin, a systematic theologian who presented his theology in a neatly organized and presented list of theological topics. Instead, he was a pastoral and practical theologian who more often than not responded to a pastoral need or doctrinal question on an "as-needed" basis. Thus, we do not have a simple statement from Luther that says, "here is what I think faith is." Instead, we must read what he says about faith in order to understand what he meant when he used the word.

The first thing we should note is the word itself that Luther uses when he speaks of faith. In German he used the word *glauben* which means both "to believe" and "to trust." *Glauben* was a perfect choice for Luther because for him faith is fundamentally a relationship between God and man. A relationship is built on more than just believing; it is built on trust. Thus, for Luther, when one has faith in God's promises one trusts God. It is more than just believing that

---

7 *LW* 34: 336–7; emphasis added.

God's promises are real or that God's word in scripture can be believed to be true. In 1535, Luther wrote that "faith grasps hold of Christ, who died for our sins and arose again for our justification."[8] Floundering in a sea of sin, a Christian grasps hold of Christ like a man drowning in the ocean would grasp hold of a life raft. The difference however is that while faith grasps hold of Christ, Christ also grasps the sinner. Holding onto Christ is a gift from God:

> Look here! This is how you must cultivate Christ in yourself, and see how in him God holds before you his mercy and offers it to you without any prior merits of your own. It is from such a view of his grace that you must draw faith and confidence in the forgiveness of all your sins. Faith, therefore, does not originate in works; neither do works create faith, but faith must spring up and flow from the blood and wounds and death of Christ. If you see in these that God is so kindly disposed toward you that he even gives his own Son for you, then your heart in turn must grow sweet and disposed toward God. And in this way your confidence must grow out of pure good will and love—God's toward you, and yours toward God. We never read that the Holy Spirit was given to anybody because he had performed some works, but always when men have heard the gospel of Christ and the mercy of God.[9]

The essence of faith for Luther is trusting God and allowing God to be God. The content of faith is the forgiveness of sins. Faith and justification are intimately linked for Luther.

This aspect of faith, a faith that "cleanses through the remission of sins" is Luther's understanding of alien righteousness or the imputation of righteousness.[10] According to Luther, faith comes to us as a gift of God through the hearing of God's judgment (the Law) and then God's grace (the Gospel). The law of God alerts us that we cannot do anything to earn our own salvation. When one considers the Ten Commandments or the Sermon on the Mount in Matthew, all fall short of the requirements of righteousness. Thus,

---

8 Luther, "Theses on Faith" (1535), *LW* 34: 110; *WA* 39: 45. Translation altered.

9 Luther, *Treatise on Good Works* (1520), *LW* 44: 38.

10 Luther, "Disputation on Justification" (1536), *LW* 31: 168.

the Law leaves us bereft of hope. It is in that hopelessness that God comes to humanity in the promise of the Gospel. When faith is awakened it grasps hold of this promise and finds forgiveness where there truly should not be any. As early as his lectures on Romans, Luther wrote, "Therefore we are righteous outwardly when we are righteous solely through the imputation of God and not of ourselves or our own work."[11] The righteousness that judges a sinner saved, therefore, is not a quality trait of a person as that person.[12] It is completely and totally new condition. The easiest way to think of this imputation of righteousness, or declaration of righteousness, is to think of God looking at a sinner and then saying "Because of what Christ has done on your behalf, you are now forgiven." Or in Luther's own words, "God imputes the righteousness of faith freely through His mercy, for the sake of Christ."[13]

For Luther then, the Christian stands before God forgiven even while he is a sinner. This is the key idea behind his statement that Christians are *simul iustus et peccator.* The phrase first appears, again, in his lectures on Romans. *Simul iustus et peccator* means "simultaneously saint (or forgiven) and sinner." It is one of the true benchmarks of his theology. Luther was raised and educated in a system that sought each day to create "better Christians." These better Christians would decrease the amount of sin in their lives and thereby increase the amount of merit they earned from God toward their salvation. Luther, however, argued that this amounted to works righteousness. Instead, Luther argued that before God we will always remain a sinner.[14] We will always deserve judgment. We will never earn salvation. Instead, salvation is a gift to be received not a standard to be achieved. This does not mean that a Christian could not, or should not, do good deeds. Indeed people should do charitable and noble works according to Luther. But those acts do not earn one salvation.

---

11 Luther, *Lectures on Romans* (1515/1516), *LW* 25: 257.
12 Luther, *Lectures on Galatians* (1531), *LW* 26: 166: "Christian righteousness is, namely, that righteousness by which Christ lives in us, not the righteousness that is in our own person."
13 Luther, *Lectures on Galatians* (1531), *LW* 26: 123.
14 Luther, "Disputation Concerning Justification" (1536), *LW* 34: 151: "Therefore, whoever is justified is still a sinner; and yet he is considered fully and perfectly righteous by God who pardons and is merciful."

Forgiveness is, as we have seen, not the only thing given in Luther's understanding of justification by faith alone. Christ himself is present in faith, "through faith Christ dwells in a person and pours his grace into him, through which it comes about that a person is governed, not by his own spirit but by Christ's."[15]

THE FINNISH SCHOOL

Recently, there has been an increasing amount of confusion regarding the indwelling of Christ in Luther's theology and its implications for his understanding of justification because of the work of a number of Finnish theologians. The Finnish interpretation of Luther or the so-called Finnish School is centered on the work of Tuomo Mannermaa and his students. In 1979, Mannermaa (at the time a professor of Church History at the University of Helsinki) published *In ipsa fide Christus adest: Luterilaisen ja ortodoksisen kritinuskonkäsityksen leikkauspiste* (In Faith Itself is Christ Really Present: The Point of Intersection between Lutheran and Orthodox Theology).[16] The advent of the Finnish School was based in part on the hope of finding a common ground in ecumenical dialogues between Lutheran and Orthodox churches. Mannermaa argues that the focus on forensic or passive justification overshadows an equally important aspect of Luther's understanding of justification. Mannermaa believes that Luther pays at least as much attention to idea that justification is a real indwelling of Christ in the sinner that transforms the believer through a process of *theosis* or deification. As we have already seen, Luther does discuss Christ indwelling the justified Christian. What Luther does not discuss beyond a few rare quotations is the deification of the Christian or the word *theosis*. However, if one does emphasize these rare quotations, a more ecumenically useful Luther emerges because of the active theologies of *theosis* in both Roman Catholicism and the Orthodox communion.

Largely because of its usefulness in ecumenical dialogues, the Finnish interpretation has developed a significant following among

---

15 Luther, *Lectures on Galatians*, *LW* 27: 238.
16 It was translated into German in 1989 and into English in 2005 as *Christ Present in Faith: Luther's View of Justification*. The delay in translation has meant that the impact of the Finnish School was not truly felt until the 1990s.

American theologians; primary among them are Carl E. Braaten, Robert W. Jenson, and David S. Yeago. The Finns have also garnered their fair share of critics. Criticism most often comes from church historians like Timothy Wengert who notes that this reading of Luther is not "new nor, in the final analysis, [is it] germane to the heart of Luther's theology."[17] For example, Julius Köstlin discussed Christ's indwelling in the mid-nineteenth century.[18] What Köstlin recognized and the Finnish School diminishes is the fact that for Luther the indwelling of Christ was a gift of the Holy Spirit as a consequence of justification by faith alone and is a part of Luther's understanding of the work of sanctification. It cannot be seen as an alternative to forensic justification.[19]

CONCLUSION

The centrality of justification by faith in the theology of Martin Luther has been widely recognized since the sixteenth century. In 1531, as he sought to defend the new Lutheran confession of faith, the *Augsburg Confession*, Luther's colleague Philip Melanchthon noted that justification was "main doctrine of Christianity."[20] Luther himself called it the doctrine upon which "the church stands or

---

17 Timothy J. Wengert, "Review of *Union with Christ*," in *Theology Today* 56/3 (1999), 433.

18 Julius Köstlin, *Luthers Theologie in Ihrer Geschichtlichen Entwicklung Und Ihrem Inneren Zusammenhange*, 2 vols. (Stuttgart: J. F. Steinkopf, 1863), II: 446. Julius Köstlin, *The Theology of Luther in Its Historical Development and Inner Harmony*, trans. Charles E. Hay, 2 vols. (Philadelphia: Lutheran Publication Society, 1897), II: 438.

19 See, Formula of Concord, Solid Declaration III, "Concerning the Righteousness of Faith before God," in Robert Kolb and Timothy Wengert, eds., *The Book of Concord* (Minneapolis: Fortress Press, 2000), 572. "However, this indwelling of God is not the righteousness of faith, which St. Paul treats and calls *iustitia Dei* (that is, the righteousness of God), for the sake of which we are pronounced righteous before God. Rather, this indwelling is the result of the righteousness of faith which precedes it, and this righteousness [of faith] is nothing else than the forgiveness of sins and the acceptance of poor sinners by grace, only because of Christ's obedience and merit."

20 Philip Melanchthon, *Apology for the Augsburg Confession*, IV.2 in Theodore G. Tappert, ed., *The Book of Concord: The Confessions of the Evangelical Lutheran Church* (Philadelphia: Fortress Press, 1959), 107.

falls."[21] In 1577, as his followers sought to heal a number of theological disputes that arose following his death, they quoted both Melanchthon and Luther in order to declare on behalf of the Lutheran church that justification by faith was "chief article of all Christian doctrine."[22] Ultimately, even one of the main supporters of the Finnish School calls it the "chief article of faith of classical Reformation theology."[23]

---

21 *WA* 40[III]: 335.
22 Formula of Concord, Solid Declaration III, "Concerning the Righteousness of Faith before God," in Tappert, ed., *The Book of Concord: The Confessions of the Evangelical Lutheran Church*, 539.
23 Veli-Matti Kärkkäinen, *One with God: Salvation as Deification and Justification* (Collegeville, MN: Liturgical Press, 2004), 10.

CHAPTER 4

THE LAW, THE GOSPEL, AND THE CROSS: THEMES IN LUTHER'S THEOLOGY

In 1529, Martin Luther and Lucas Cranach worked together, as they had often in the past, on a new image that would help spread Luther's message. The image, which was later copied in paintings and in sanctuary altar pieces, is divided by a tree into two halves. On the left side, the tree is dead, on the right side is alive and growing. The left side illustrates Luther's conception of the Law. The top of the picture features Christ upon the judgment seat. Below him, Adam and Eve stand at the Tree with the serpent whispering to Eve. In the foreground, Moses and Prophets point to the Ten Commandments. The center of the picture is dominated by Death and the Devil as they prod a naked man (who represents all men) toward the fires of hell. On the right side, Christ is upon the cross rather than the judgment seat. John the Baptist points the naked man to Christ upon the cross and grace pours out of Christ's side onto the naked man. In foreground of the picture, where Moses stands with the Law on the opposite side, a resurrected Christ emerges from the tomb and crushes Death and the Devil under his feet. The imagery is as clear as it is stark: relying on the Law for salvation will only lead to damnation. Salvation can only come through Christ.

The print was named *Gesetz und Gnade* (literally, Law and Grace) (Figure 4.1) and is widely known in English as Law and Gospel. For Luther, properly distinguishing between the Law and the Gospel was fundamental to all theology. In 1521, while writing a brief exposition of Matthew 11 (where Jesus is speaking to the disciples of John the Baptist about his work and the proclamation of the Gospel), Luther says that "Almost all scripture and all knowledge of theology depend

Figure 4.1 Image of the Law and Gospel by Lucas Cranach the Elder, 1530.

upon the correct understanding of Law and Gospel."[1] Looking at the painting, even just thinking about the words Law and the Gospel as they relate to the Bible, it is easy to jump to the conclusion that Luther understood the proper distinction between them to be the difference between the Old Testament and the New Testament. Many of the images on the Law side of the picture do come from the Old Testament. As if understanding that this is a natural assumption to make, Luther heads off such speculation almost immediately. At the top of the picture, he had two scriptural quotations inscribed. One might assume that on the left hand side would be a quote from Moses or one of the Prophets. Instead, Paul declares, "For the wrath of God is revealed from heaven against all ungodliness and unrighteousness of men" (Rom. 1.18, KJV). Above the Gospel, one might expect John 3.16, instead Isaiah proclaims, "The Lord himself shall give you a sign; 'Behold, a virgin shall conceive, and bear a son'" (Isa. 7.14, KJV). If the Law and the Gospel are not the Old versus the New Testament, what exactly does Luther mean when he says that we must have a correct understanding of them?

---

1 *WA* 7: 502.

THE THEOLOGICAL USE OF THE LAW

Distinguishing between the Law and the Gospel was, even in Luther's day, a fairly established theological construct. However, many theologians followed Augustine and looked at the Law and Gospel as successive orders of God's work in the world. The Law came with Moses and was fulfilled and overcome by Christ. There is certainly, also, a Pauline sense to this interpretation. Luther, however, did not see the Law and Gospel in this light. Rather than successive modes of God's work in the world, he saw them as a paradoxical pair that worked in concert with each other.

The most important way in which the Law and the Gospel work together is in justification. Luther explains this working together,

When the Law shows us our sin, our past life immediately comes to our mind. Then the sinner, in his great anguish of mind, groans and says to himself: "Oh, how damnably I have lived! If only I could live longer! Then I would amend my life." Thus human reason cannot refrain from looking at active righteousness, that is, its own righteousness; nor can it shift its gaze to passive, that is, Christian righteousness, but it simply rests in the active righteousness. So deeply is this evil rooted in us, and so completely have we acquired this unhappy habit! Taking advantage of the weakness of our nature, Satan increases and aggravates these thoughts in us. Then it is impossible for the conscience to avoid being more seriously troubled, confounded, and frightened. For it is impossible for the human mind to conceive any comfort of itself, or to look only at grace amid its consciousness and terror of sin, or consistently to reject all discussion of works. To do this is beyond human power and thought. Indeed, it is even beyond the Law of God. For although the Law is the best of all things in the world, it still cannot bring peace to a terrified conscience but makes it even sadder and drives it to despair. For by the Law sin becomes exceedingly sinful (Rom. 7:13).

Therefore the afflicted conscience has no remedy against despair and eternal death except to take hold of the promise of grace offered in Christ[2]

---

2 *Lectures on Galatians, LW* 26: 5. The entire lectures are found in *LW* 26–7 or *WA* 40^I–0^{II}. The Galatians Lectures were first published in 1535 in

Thus, the Law works when it confronts us with our sinful ways. The Law reveals the utter futility of salvation by works. The Law cannot save because it is only experienced as judgment. It condemns sin and kills the sinner so that he or she may then come alive in Christ.[3] It is therefore a helpmate to the Gospel:

> Now, when sins are unrecognized, there is no room for a remedy and no hope of a cure, because men will not submit to the touch of a healer when they imagine themselves well and in no need of a physician. Therefore, the Law is necessary to make sin known so that when its gravity and magnitude are recognized, man in his pride who imagines himself well may be humbled and may sigh and gasp for the grace that is offered in Christ.[4]

This is what Luther means when he argues that one must have a correct understanding of the Gospel. When the distinction is properly understood, we can see that the Law aids salvation.

When it is incorrectly understood it becomes a terror (as Luther understood all too well from his own *Anfechtungen*). As Cranach's illustration demonstrates graphically, if one confuses the Law and the Gospel and views the Law as the proper avenue for achieving salvation then it aids the devil in his work. Incorrectly understanding the Law aids the devil because what should be helpmate to salvation (the recognition that we cannot save ourselves) has become a hindrance. Despair rules when the Law is confused with Gospel because there is

---

Wittenberg by Johann Luft. They were first translated into English in 1575 and remained a popular work that was repeatedly printed. The coverpage of the English translation makes clear that many in the sixteenth century already appreciated the significance of the work and its central motif: *A Commentarie of M. Doctor Martin Luther Upon the Epistle of S. Paul to the Galathians, first collected and gathered word by word out of his preaching, and now out of Latine faithfully translated into English for the unlearned. Wherein is set forth most excellently the glorious riches of Gods grace and the power of the gospel, with the difference betwene the law and the gospel, and strength of faith declared: to the joyfull comfort and confirmation of all true Christian beleavers.*

3 Luther, *Concerning the Letter and the Spirit* (1521) *LW* 39: 186: "Therefore it is impossible for someone who does not first hear the Law and let himself be killed by the letter to hear the Gospel and let the grace of the Spirit bring him to life. Grace is only given to those who long for it. Life is a help only to those who are dead, grace only to sin, the Spirit only to the letter."
4 Luther, *The Bondage of the Will* (1525), *LW* 33: 261.

no way to find a gracious God when the Law alone guides one's life before God. The sinner has given up Christ and in so doing has lost all hope of salvation. John the Baptist reminds the sinner that works will never suffice. Only Christ's sacrifice on the cross will open salvation to the sinner.

Thus, a sinner's hope is found only in the good news of the crucified Christ. The late American theologian Gerhard Forde noted that the distinction between the Law and the Gospel can sometimes best be seen in the different types of speech that typify them. Whereas Law is spoken in imperative speech, for example, "Thou shalt not murder," the Gospel is best spoken in declarative statements like "There is therefore now no condemnation for those who are in Christ Jesus."[5] At its most basic level, the proclamation of the Gospel must be discerned from the Law because it is a declaration that the sinner is accepted by God as a saint. Death has been crushed by the cross and the resurrection. Again, we return to Luther's *Lectures on Galatians*:

> But where Christ is truly seen, there there must be full and perfect joy in the Lord and peace of heart, where the heart declares: "Although I am a sinner according to the Law, judged by the righteousness of the Law, nevertheless I do not despair. I do not die, because Christ lives who is my righteousness and my eternal and heavenly life. In that righteousness and life I have no sin, conscience, and death. I am indeed a sinner according to the present life and its righteousness, as a son of Adam where the Law accuses me, death reigns and devours me. But above this life I have another righteousness, another life, which is Christ, the Son of God, who does not know sin and death but is righteousness and eternal life. For His sake this body of mine will be raised from the dead and delivered from the slavery of the Law and sin, and will be sanctified together with the spirit."[6]

THE POLITICAL USE OF THE LAW

Properly distinguishing or understanding the difference between the Law and the Gospel has a second side to it beyond justification.

---

5 Gerhard Forde, "Law and Gospel in Luther's Hermeneutic," *Interpretation* 37 (1983), 241.

6 *LW* 26: 8.

Paradoxically, this is often called the "First Use of the Law."[7] It comes second here because for Luther, as a biblical theologian, the "Second Use" was always far more important. This does not mean, however, that Luther did not believe the civil use of the law had an essential role to play in human existence. In fact, quite the opposite. Luther believed that the first use of the law was established by God for the benefit of human society. The first use of the Law is as an aid to creation in that it limits human sin and avarice and promotes the common good. Therefore, it is a crucial part of God's plan for the ordering of creation. It limits the work of the devil in the world by curbing sin and malfeasance. To do this it utilizes both judgment and punishment:

> [God] has subjected [the wicked] to the sword so that, even though they would like to, they are unable to practice their wickedness, and if they do practice it they cannot do so without fear or with success and impunity.[8]

The political use of the law is established first in families.[9] Parents instruct their children in right and wrong and acceptable versus unacceptable behavior. For Luther all civil or political authority is established first in the proper ordering of the home. In a properly ordered home parents use instruction, correction (judgment), and punishment to train their children in correct behavior. A properly ordered home allows children to be raised in both safety and security. The same can be said about larger human communities (whether a village, a city, or a nation). Writing on the Commandment to honor parents Luther says,

---

7 For example, the 1577 *Formula of Concord* discusses three uses of the law: political, soteriological, and regenerative. Theodore G. Tappert, *The Book of Concord : The Confessions of the Evangelical Lutheran Church* (Philadelphia: Fortress Press, 1959), 479: The law has been given to men for three reasons: (1) to maintain external discipline against unruly and disobedient men, (2) to lead men to a knowledge of their sin, (3) after they are reborn, and although the flesh still inheres in them, to give them on that account a definite rule according to which they should pattern and regulate their entire life. It is concerning the third function of the law that a controversy has arisen among a few theologian.

8 Luther, *On Temporal Authority* (1523), *LW* 45: 91.

9 *LW* 1: 103, "After the church has been established, the household government is also set up, when Eve is added to Adam as his companion."

But what is said and commanded of parents must also be understood of those who, when the parents are dead or not there, take their place, such as friends, relatives, godparents, temporal lords, and spiritual fathers. For everybody must be ruled and subject to other men. So we see here again how many good works are taught in this commandment, for in it all our life is made subject to other men. That is the reason obedience is so highly praised, and all virtue and good works are included in it.[10]

When civil society is governed by laws, justice (judgment), and reasonable punishment of lawbreakers human communities thrive. However, just as salvation is jeopardized when the Law and the Gospel are confused theologically, civil life is also jeopardized when the two are confused politically.

When they become confused politically, people begin to believe that perhaps the Gospel ought to order life in the civil community. Luther believed this was one of the most significant dangers of Anabaptism, whether in its crusading paradigm or its anchoritic paradigm.[11] In the first case, perhaps best epitomized by Thomas Müntzer, the world is forced to conform to the Gospel in all aspects. Those who opposed Müntzer's understanding of the Gospel's demand were deemed enemies of God. In 1524, Müntzer described in a sermon before Saxony's princes his vision of Law and Gospel:

Now if you are to be true rulers you must seize the very roots of government, following the command of Christ. Drive his enemies away from the elect; you are the instruments to do this. My friend,

---

10 *LW* 44: 82. See also, 54: 67, "It can be shown by proof that the magistracy is based on the Fourth Commandment. The reason is that obedience is necessary. The authority of parents is also necessary. If, then, the authority of parents vanishes and the obedience of children increases, it's according to natural law that the children have a guardian to help bring them up. Such guardians are the governing authorities, and the emperor is therefore the guardian of all parents."

11 A crusading theologian seeks to enforce his view of theology and godly living both through preaching and the use of force. An anchoritic theologian seeks, like ancient anchorite monks who lived alone in the desert, to withdraw from the wider world into a homogeneous community. For a fuller discussion of the various types of political theology in the sixteenth century please see, David M. Whitford, "Robbing Paul to Pay Peter," in *Paul in the Sixteenth Century*, ed. R. Ward Holder (Leiden: Brill, 2009).

don't let us have any of these hackneyed posturings about the power of God achieving everything without any resort to your sword; otherwise it may rust in its scabbard. Would that this could happen! Whatever any scholar may say, Christ speaks clearly enough in Matthew 7, John 15: "Any tree which does not produce good fruit should be rooted out and thrown in the fire." . . . Do not, therefore, allow the evil-doers, who turn us away from God to continue living . . . St. Paul thinks the same, when he says of the sword that it is set in the hands of the rulers to exact vengeance on the evil and give protection to the good, Romans 13.[12]

Luther believed that such a co-mixing of Law and Gospel jeopardized both the true proclamation of the Gospel and the necessary work of the Law. It reified the day-in and day-out activities of a civil community. Reification grants to political questions a quality they do not deserve and that is not helpful. It allows one to demonize one's opposition and undermines the pragmatic nature of politics and governance.[13]

Anchoritic theologians were similar to Thomas Müntzer in that they sought to govern their common life solely by the dictates of scripture but did so in separated communities distinct from the larger society as a whole. They believed that the civil law was not necessary for Christians. The temporal law exists to curb the sinfulness of non-Christians. For a wayward Christian, those who according to the Schleitheim Confession "somehow slip and fall into error," all that was needed (or in fact allowed by scripture) was the ban. In this type of community, the ban functioned to limit the erring member's contact with the faith community until such time that the wayward Christian might be welcomed back into full communion with the community. Luther believed that this perspective was terribly naïve. The power of sin is vastly underestimated.[14] The world is populated with sinners and the wicked. The truly just are a minority. To believe that just because a community says it is a Christian community makes it so is absurd. Discerning "true" Christians from "false" Christians

---

12 Thomas Müntzer, *The Collected Works of Thomas Müntzer*, translated and edited by Peter Matheson (Edinburgh: T & T Clark, 1988), 247–8.
13 Please see Chapter 8 for a fuller discussion of Luther's reaction to Thomas Müntzer and the Peasants' War.
14 Please see Chapter 5 on Luther's understanding of the bondage of the human will.

is a game of folly. To those who believe that they can live in a world without civil laws, Luther replies wryly, "Take heed and first fill the world with real Christians before you attempt to rule it in a Christian and evangelical manner."[15]

THE THEOLOGY OF THE CROSS

The proper distinction between the Law and the Gospel is one of the most important motifs running throughout Luther's theology. A second equally important motif is the proper distinction between a theology of glory and a theology of the cross. The distinction between a theology of glory and a theology of the cross was first articulated by Luther in 1518. In September of 1517, before the firestorm that was the *Ninety-Five Theses*, Luther wrote another set of theses for disputation among his students at the University of Wittenberg. The subject of the disputation was the nature and efficacy of scholastic theology. It is, in many ways, a more theologically radical document than the *Ninety-Five* but does not touch on money the way indulgences did in the *Ninety-Five* and so met with rather less fanfare. At a number of points in the disputation, Luther categorically rejects the use of Aristotle in theology. In thesis 40 he writes, "no one can become a theologian unless he becomes one without Aristotle." He also rejects the idea of human merit in salvation writing, "Hope does not grow out of merit but out of suffering which destroys merit." In this disputation, we can see many early hallmarks of Luther's theology: it rejects works, it focuses on faith, and it is centered on revelation as the source of theology as opposed to logic or philosophy. When Luther was called to explain himself and his theology in April 1518 at a meeting of his monastic order in Heidelberg, he chose to return to the themes expressed in the September 1517 disputation rather than its more famous October cousin.

The Heidelberg Catechism begins by discussing the difference between the Law and the Gospel and Luther notes that the Law cannot "advance man on his way to righteousness." After discussing the Law and the Gospel, he moves on to consider the futility of works righteousness. In thesis 18, he notes that the only way to God is grace, "a man must utterly despair his own ability before he is prepared to receive the gift of grace." What Luther has been doing up through

---

15 *LW* 45: 91.

thesis 18 is setting up a dichotomy between the works of men and the work of God; the foolishness of the cross versus the supposed wisdom of human logic, experience, philosophy.[16] As he moves to thesis 19, his language gets more vague but the pattern of the "Theology of the Cross," begins to come into focus. According to Luther, God works in ways that human wisdom cannot comprehend; he calls these the "invisible things of God." Only faith can perceive the invisible things of God. Man, as man, cannot comprehend or understand how God works in the world. God must reveal himself to humanity. However, unlike scholastic theologians who in general saw a continuity between God's self-revelation and human perception, Luther argues that revelation is indirect and concealed in the places where one least expects to find God. Because of humanity's fallen condition, one cannot see God face-to-face. In thesis 20, Luther clarifies what this means. Thesis 20 is often translated into English, "He deserves to be called a theologian, however, who comprehends the visible and manifest things of God seen through suffering and the cross."[17] The middle section is very important and difficult to translate elegantly into English which is why translators often choose "visible and manifest." The Latin actually reads, "*visibilia et posteriora Dei.*" A literal translation would read the "visible and posterior (or backside) of God." This is, indeed, an inelegant translation, but Luther is not looking for worldly elegance in this thesis and the visible backside of God is important to him. It is an allusion to Exodus 33, where Moses seeks to see the Glory of the Lord but instead sees only the backside. For Luther, no one, no theologian especially, can see God face-to-face and live; so God reveals himself on the backside, that is to say, where it seems he should not be. This means in and through the human nature of Christ, in his weakness, his suffering, and his foolishness.[18]

---

16 Jos E. Vercruyse in "Gesetz und Liebe, Die Struktur der 'Heidelberg Disputation' Luthers [1518]," *Lutherjahrbuch* 48 (1981), 11–12, vividly demonstrates this dichotomy by placing theses 3 and 4 side by side:

3. The Works of Humans	4. The Works of God
Always look splendid	Always look deformed
Appear to be good	Appear to be bad
Are nevertheless in all probability	Are nevertheless in very truth
Mortal sins	Immortal merits

17 *LW* 31: 40.

18 In his explanation for thesis 20, he writes, "Now it is not sufficient for anyone, and it does him no good to recognize God in his glory and

The distinctions between the works of men and the work of God and a theology that thinks it perceives God in his majesty rather than a theology that does perceive God in the suffering of the cross is the foundation of what Luther calls the primary distinction between theologians of glory and theologians of the cross. As one might surmise, Luther does not believe that a theologian of glory is truly a theologian at all. Instead, they "call evil good and good evil." They miss the point of theology which is to describe God as he actually *is* rather than as we might wish him to be. "That wisdom which sees the invisible things of God in works as perceived by man is completely puffed up, blinded, and hardened."[19] The theology of the cross will weave a thread through many of Luther's later theological works including, for example, his important work on the bondage of the will against Erasmus. The study of Luther's theology of the cross began in earnest with Walter von Loewenich's 1929 *Luthers Theologia Crucis*. Loewenich would edit and revise the text a number of times and the fifth edition of the work was translated in 1976.[20] Anyone seeking to understand the theology of the cross ought to begin with Loewenich first. The British Methodist, Philip S. Watson, used the theology of the cross as one of the important aspects that defined what Watson called Luther's Copernican revolution in theology.[21] More recently, Alister McGrath published a study on Luther's use of the theology of the cross in 1985. That work offers many insights but is, in many ways, a recapitulation of Loewenich. In 1997, Gerhard Forde published *On Being a Theologian of the Cross*, which is a detailed theological study of the Heidelberg Catechism.[22] It puts Luther's theology in context and then into conversation with modern theological issues and struggles.

---

majesty, unless he recognizes him in the humility and shame of the cross." *LW* 31: 52.

19 *LW* 31: 41. Thesis 22.

20 Walter von Loewenich, *Luther's Theology of the Cross*, trans. Herbert J. A. Bouman (Minneapolis: Augsburg, 1976); Walter von Loewenich, *Luthers Theologia Crucis* (Munich: Kaiser, 1929).

21 Philip Watson, *Let God Be God* (London: Epworth Press, 1947).

22 Gerhard O. Forde, *On Being a Theologian of the Cross: Reflections on Luther's Heidelberg Disputation, 1518* (Grand Rapids: Eerdmans, 1997).

CONCLUSION

Understanding how Luther used paradox and dichotomy is an important element in making Luther less perplexing and bewildering. He was not, on many levels, a systematic theologian who sought to make theology fit into neatly ordered schemes and classifications. He was certainly not a linear theologian. Instead he often thought his way around a theological issue looking at it from many different sides and from different perspectives. He was comfortable with paradox and this is why he is so perplexing. But if one allows oneself to sit inside his theology and become comfortable with his use of paradox and dichotomy, then one can begin to glimpse the genius of his work and what he believed was at the center of all theology: the ultimate of theological paradoxes—the Incarnation—that God became Man and lived among us. That foundational paradox drove him to see that all theology, indeed all revelation, is paradoxical.

CHAPTER 5

THE BONDAGE OF THE WILL

In 1537, Martin Luther was perhaps the most famous man in Europe. He was 53 and the undisputed leader of Protestantism. Others also recognized his significance and so presented him with the idea of collecting all his works and publishing them. He did not think that a wise decision. Whether humility or a genuine uncertainty about the long-term significance of many of his works led to this opinion we are unable to tell. However, in a letter to a colleague in southern Germany, Luther noted that he did find two of his works to be of lasting importance the treatise on the bondage of the will and his catechism.[1] A great many students who have read the treatise *De Servo Arbitrio* have not shared his esteem for the work. In fact, it is often regarded as one of the most difficult to understand of all his writings. *De Servo Arbitrio* was written in 1525 and was an answer to a tract on the power and efficacy of the human will written by Desiderius Erasmus in 1524. In English, Luther's tract has been called *The Bondage of the Will*, since it was first translated in 1823. The title does not actually say that, however. The actual title is *On Bound* (or *Enslaved*) *Choice*, the difference is subtle and yet as we shall see, significant.

PICKING A FIGHT: DESIDERIUS ERASMUS AND LUTHER

When Martin Luther posted the *Ninety-Five Theses* he did so as an unknown junior professor at a small German university. At the same time, Desiderius Erasmus (1466–1536) was already northern Europe's greatest and most famous scholar. He had by that time taught at

---

1 *LW* 50: 171–2.

Cambridge, served as personal tutor to Charles Hapsburg, prince of Spain, grandson of Emperor Maximilian, and the future Holy Roman Emperor, and he had published his first edition of the Greek New Testament, *Novum Instrumentum*.[2] He was close friends with Thomas More and a treasured dinner guest at the finest tables of Europe. In other words, Luther and Erasmus did not travel in the same circles. Nevertheless, Erasmus would be drawn into the Luther Affair repeatedly and from his perspective increasingly dangerously.

Erasmus first learned of Luther in 1516, though most likely he did not know his name. Luther had received a copy of Erasmus's *Novum Instrumentum* in 1516 and profited by it almost daily. Many of his theological suspicions found confirmation in Erasmus's Greek New Testament. At the same time, Luther had misgivings about the orientation of Erasmus's theology. Specifically, he had concerns about Erasmus's reading of Romans 9 and his dependence upon St. Jerome rather than St. Augustine. The question that vexed Luther was the degree to which people had to follow the Laws of Moses in order to be saved. Erasmus had argued that when Paul condemned the idea of a "righteousness of works," he was only speaking of certain ceremonial aspects of the Law. Luther disagreed. He believed that there was no righteousness in works outside of those done in faith. He wrote to his friend George Spalatin, "If good works are performed outside of faith in Christ [*extra fidem Christi*] then they can make a man a Fabricus or Regulus, even a blameless man among men. Nevertheless, they have as little in common with righteousness as apples have to figs."[3] He asked Spalatin to send this critique to Erasmus. Spalatin did but also chose not to include Luther's name and instead said that a certain "Augustinian friar" had raised this issue. Erasmus seems to have ignored the critique. That is not unusual because nearly everyday he was receiving letters from men across Europe attempting to engage him in theological debate or to simply ask a question. He could not answer them all.

A year later when the *Ninety-Five Theses* became famous Erasmus might have remembered the letter from Spalatin, but if he did he did

---

2 Only the first edition was called *Novum Instrumentum*, the others were all titled *Novum Testamentum*.

3 *WABR* 1: 70–1. Fabricus and Regulus in this sentence refer to heroes from ancient Rome.

not hold a grudge against the young professor. Instead his initial interpretation of the *Theses* was positive but also reflected his general tendency to hold his judgments close. He sent copies of the *Theses* to friends in England and wrote approvingly of them to his colleague Johann Lang in 1518. Indeed, Erasmus would have found much to like in Luther's early work. In his famous *Praise of Folly* from 1509, Erasmus had criticized many of the abuses that Luther rejected, including the selling of indulgences. At the same time, Luther was reaching out to Erasmus in the hope of winning an ally for the Reformation cause. Luther was abnormally courteous (bordering even on the obsequious) in his first-ever letter directly to Erasmus. He wrote,

> Where is there someone whose heart Erasmus does not occupy, whom Erasmus does not teach, over whom Erasmus does not hold sway? . . . I have heard from the excellent Fabricus Capito that you are acquainted with my name through my writings on indulgences that are truly not even worth mentioning. I also realize from your preface to the latest edition of the *Enchiridion* that you not only know but also approve of my musings. Therefore I feel compelled to acknowledge (even if in a most primitive letter) your outstanding spirit, which has enriched my own and that of all others . . . As a result, my Erasmus, amiable man, if it seems acceptable to you, acknowledge also this little brother in Christ.[4]

Erasmus had, in fact, written an approving line in the 1518 revised edition of his *Enchiridion*. In a new preface, written as a letter to Paul Volz, Erasmus wrote that "if someone admonished us saying, for example, that it would be safer to put more trust in good works than in papal dispensations, one is not condemning his dispensations in any case, but preferring what according to Christ's teaching is more reliable."[5] Here Erasmus was clearly making reference to theses 43 and 45 from the *Ninety-Five Theses* where Luther writes, "Christians are to be taught that he who gives to the poor or lends money to the

---

4 *LW* 48: 118. Translation altered. Compare to *WABR* 1: 361–3.
5 Desiderius Erasmus, "Preface to Paul Volz" (1518), in *Handbook of the Militant Christian*, *CWE* 66: 18. Translation altered. Compare to *Opus Epistolarum Des. Erasmi Roterdami*, edited by P. S. Allen. 3: 372.

needy does a better deed than he who buys indulgences."[6] Erasmus, however, had not read everything Luther had written to this point and once he did, he began to have significant misgivings about the totality of Luther's thought. In that vein, he wrote to Archbishop Albrecht of Mainz stating that he believed that Luther was "overly rash." He also wrote to his Basel printer, Johann Froben encouraging him to stop publishing the works of Luther. Despite his misgivings, Erasmus refused to join in open condemnation of Luther. For example, in 1520, while he was in residence at the University of Louvain, the theology faculty wrote and published a condemnation of Luther's theology. Erasmus was urged to join their condemnation. He did not. A few months later, when Luther replied to their condemnation, he wrote that the theologians didn't just condemn him but also Ockham, the "Scholastic Fathers," Johannes Pico Mirandola, Lorenzo Valla, Johannes Reuchlin, Jacques Lefèvre d'Étaples, and even "Erasmus, that ram caught in the brier by the horns."[7] Erasmus seems to have approved of Luther's assertions but wished that he had left his name out of the discussion. By the early 1520s, Erasmus was widely seen as a forerunner (or even the ghost writer for) Luther. A common saying at the time asserted that "Erasmus laid the egg that Luther hatched." At the Diet of Worms, the papal legate Aleander wrote that, "Erasmus is the source of all this [meaning Luther's] heresy."[8] Pressure was mounting for Erasmus to choose a side.

For example, in 1521 (and then again in 1523) Henry VIII of England urged Erasmus to speak out forcefully against Luther. Duke George of Albertine Saxony likewise urged him to oppose Luther. Even the emperor made similar requests. In 1523, Pope Adrian wrote his old friend Erasmus and urged him to finally rise up to defend Christianity, "Beloved son, you are a man of great learning. You are the one to refute the heresies of Martin Luther by which innumerable souls are being taken to damnation."[9] Erasmus initially attempted to avoid such a confrontation, but ultimately the will of the pontiff was

---

6 *LW* 31: 29.

7 *WA* 6: 184.

8 Hieronymus Aleander, *Die Depeschen Des Nuntius Aleander Vom Wormser Reichstage 1521* (Halle: Verein fuer Reformationsgeschichte, 1886), 48.

9 "Letter of Adrian VI to Erasmus" (Jan. 1523), quoted in Roland Bainton, *Erasmus of Christendom* (New York: Scribner, 1969), 177.

not to be ignored and in 1524, Erasmus began to set ink to paper and drive a lasting and final wedge between himself and Luther.

DE LIBERO ARBITRIO: DIATRIBE—
ON THE FREE WILL: A DIATRIBE

Before Erasmus set down to write the treatise on the Free Will, he wrote two other short treatises as almost prefatory remarks for it. The first, *On the Immense Mercy of God*, set out Erasmus's belief that mercy is to be shown to all, especially fellow Christians. Too often, Christian's turn one against another over aspects of Christian theology that are not the center of one's faith. Among those topics over which people of good faith can disagree included the efficacy of indulgences and the power of the pope. When he turns to discuss the ways in which mercy ought to guide the lives of all Christians, he lifts up what is for him the essence of Christianity, "The mercy of God came to us when the Son of God came down to earth; let us in our turn come to him. Our most compassionate Lord bends low to absolve the woman taken in adultery, but we in our turn must lift up our hearts to him as he bends towards us."[10] The second treatise most likely sought to build on the first and help create an environment in which Erasmus could confront Luther, burnish his reputation among Catholics, and yet not totally cut himself off from the Wittenberg Reformer's friends and allies. *An Inquiry Concerning the Faith* is one of Erasmus's many colloquies and as such is a dialog between two people: an Orthodox Catholic named Aulus that represents Erasmus and a figure named Barbatus that represents Luther. Aulus examines Barbatus's theology using the Apostle's Creed as the axis around which the debate revolves. When Aulus asks, "Do you believe in God the Father Almighty, maker of heaven and earth?" Barbatus answers, "Yes, and what is also contained in heaven and earth, also in angelic spirits." Aulus seems surprised by the response and says, "You believe like a good Christian." "Do you believe Jesus was God and man?" Barbatus answers, "Mamixe" ("Absolutely!"). Throughout the dialog, Aulus seems surprised by the orthodoxy of Barbatus's faith. He says at the end of the dialog, "Even when I was in Rome, I did not find many so true in their faith." The implication of these two dialogs now becomes clear. Erasmus will set ink to paper in a debate with

---

10 *CWE* 70: 136.

Luther but it will not be over the central tenets of the faith. On the question of fidelity to Creed, both agree that Luther is a Christian. He is no heretic. What Erasmus will miss, however, is the fact that his definition of the essence of Christianity in *Immense Mercy* will differ significantly with Luther. For Erasmus the first step toward God was to "reject evil." Erasmus, here, betrays his hand regarding the essentials of Christianity and highlights the locus of the coming debate with Luther. Erasmus did not believe that his statement on the mercy of God reaching down to humanity and the response of people reaching back to God was controversial. To Luther, as we shall see, it was.

Erasmus calls his work a *diatribe*. Today, in English, we regard that word negatively and view it as a tirade. That is not what it meant in the sixteenth century. A *diatribe* was a specific type of academic writing that sought to clarify the issues under discussion, examine the implications of each side, but not reach an exact conclusion. One might best think of it as an airing of the issues. However, and this is vitally important to understand what happened next, Erasmus did not utilize a *diatribe* method. Instead he used the more medieval format of scholastic disputation. In a disputation, an author sets out a position and then examines and defends that position. This created an enormous opening for Luther who was far more experienced in this type of academic exercise than was Erasmus. As Robert Kolb notes, "Luther's entire academic training had schooled his mind in the art and practice of scholastic argumentation."[11] The weight of that difference in preparation for this debate became apparent in Luther's reply. Before we turn to that reply, however, we must first examine exactly what Erasmus argued.

Roland Bainton famously summed up the debate between Luther and Erasmus by noting that whereas Luther said "Let God be God," Erasmus said, "Let God be Good."[12] Bainton, here, does capture the essence of the debate. Erasmus chose the freedom of the will because he was at his core a man deeply concerned with the ethical formation of people. Much of what he wrote concerning the abuses in the church was directed at ethical and moral lapses. When he wrote

---

11 Robert Kolb, *Bound Choice, Election, and Wittenberg Theological Method: From Martin Luther to the Formula of Concord* (Grand Rapids, MI: Eerdmans, 2005), 24.
12 Bainton, *Erasmus of Christendom*, 190.

his *Handbook for a Militant Christian* it was with the belief that a Christian armed with prayer and knowledge might successfully resist and overcome the seduction of vice and moral laxity on the one hand and superstition on the other. When he read Luther's *Heidelberg Disputation* he was alarmed by the implications of what he read. In that disputation, Luther wrote, "Free will, after the Fall, even when doing the best that it can, commits a moral sin." To Erasmus, this seemed to create a scenario in which even good moral behavior was sinful. Even worse, to Erasmus, Luther seemed to make human beings into automatons controlled in every action by a god that made them in such a manner that they cannot do anything but sin and then condemns them for that sin. Such a god is certainly not good and was not the God that Erasmus saw in Jesus Christ.

Instead, Erasmus argues that if human beings were left in their fallen condition without the aid of God's mercy, then they would certainly be trapped in sin. However, as the life and work of Jesus make clear, God did not leave people alone in their sin. Instead, God's grace works preveniently (before) human effort and aids people as they seek to respond to God's call to reject evil and live good and godly Christian lives. That God aids the human will in salvation was not the point of controversy between Luther and Erasmus, however. What was at stake was the degree to which the human will played a role in that process of salvation. When Erasmus formally defines the freedom of the human will, this difference becomes apparent, "By free choice in this place we mean a power of the human will by which a man can apply himself to the things which lead to eternal salvation, or turn away from them."[13] While Erasmus has not stated in this quote that this is a natural ability in human beings outside of God's grace, that is what he intends. In 1518, in his paraphrase of Romans, Erasmus wrote on the human will when he commented on Romans 9. There he states, "some part depends on our own will and effort, although this part is so minor that it seems like nothing at all in comparison with the free kindness of God."[14] Though human actions might not compare with the work that God

---

13 Gordon Rupp and Philip Watson, eds., *Luther and Erasmus: Free Will and Salvation* (Philadelphia: Westminster Press, 1969), 47.

14 Desiderius Erasmus, *Paraphrases on Romans and Galatians*, trans. John B. Payne, Albert Rabil, and Warren S. Smith (Toronto: University of Toronto Press, 1984), 153 n. 15.

does, people do do something.[15] Here Erasmus highlights his view of the Fall. In the Fall, human reason and intellect are "obscured by sin but not extinguished."[16] Human beings retained some (however small) ability to cooperate with God and respond to God's call. Luther had already noticed this tendency in Erasmus. As early as 1517, Luther had noticed Erasmus's reading of Romans 9 and it raised serious questions for him. He wrote of these concerns to Johan Lang and confessed his grave concerns regarding Erasmus's understanding of salvation, "I am afraid that Erasmus does not advance the cause of Christ and the grace of God sufficiently . . . Human things way more with him than the divine . . . Just because one knows Greek and Hebrew does not make one a wise Christian . . . The judgment of one who attributes weight to man's will is different from one who knows nothing but grace."[17] Where Erasmus saw the need to maintain a choice by man, Luther saw the demand that God's grace be proclaimed. When he picked up his pen against Erasmus, this would be the point he drove home repeatedly.

DE SERVO ARBITRIO—THE BOUND WILL

The first thing one notices upon picking up Luther's response to Erasmus is its size. In 1524, Erasmus's text ran 96 pages. When Luther's response was published about a year and a half later it was 315 pages. The next thing one notices is the distinct rhetorical advantage Luther had in being the one to respond. In responding to Erasmus, he could not only present his own case but also deconstruct his opponent's argument at the same time. This he did, thoroughly.

If Erasmus approached the topic of the will as a teacher, Luther approached the subject as a pastor. Where Erasmus was concerned about the moral instruction of men and women, Luther was concerned with the care of their souls. At least those are the dichotomies that Luther saw when he looked at Erasmus. In the opening lines of the

---

15 Rupp and Watson, eds., *Luther and Erasmus: Free Will and Salvation*, 91. Here Erasmus uses an analogy of toddler being helped to walk by his father. The ability to walk (the ability to do good and follow God's commands) is dependent upon the father because he holds the child's hand and steadies him. On the other hand, "he does something" Erasmus says speaking of the child who does walk.

16 Ibid., 48.

17 *LW* 48: 40, translation altered please compare to *WABR* 1: 90.

treatise, Luther declares that he has a calling to proclaim the truth to both the "wise and the foolish." Here Luther was adopting the persona of Paul by alluding to the opening lines of the Letter to the Romans. Paul writes, "I am obligated both to Greeks and non-Greeks, both to the wise and the foolish. That is why I am so eager to preach the gospel also to you who are in Rome. For I am not ashamed of the gospel, because it is the power of God for the salvation of everyone who believes" (Rom. 1. 14–16).

When Luther approached the question of salvation, he always paid special attention to Paul's remark that it is the "power of God" that achieves our salvation. For Luther, if our salvation is to be guaranteed, the only one that guarantees it is God. He had suffered immeasurable fear and tribulation when he believed that he must earn (in however minor a fashion) his own salvation. Only when he finally believed that God established his salvation and that he could trust in God's promises alone did he find solace for his uneasy soul. This lead him to argue that in our relationship to God and in our theological understanding of salvation we must see that it is God who saves and we must trust him when he promises to save us.

A corollary of the assertion that it is God who saves is the belief that no works, no matter how good or, frankly, evil, can determine our salvation. It is God who saves. Thus, when Luther wrote in Heidelberg that "Free will, after the Fall, even when doing the best that it can, commits a moral sin" he did not mean that men and women cannot do good things. He did not deny that people could come to the aid of those in peril or those less fortunate and that those things are somehow sinful. What he meant was that those good acts, as good as they are cannot ever be salvific. They have no affect on justification whatsoever. Thus viewed salvifically, they remain sinful. This is difficult to understand, certainly, but Luther also believed that good acts could and often did arise not out of care for the other but out of a self-serving interest in earning salvation. Thus what appears from the outside to be a good deed turns out to be a selfish and therefore sinful act.

Here Luther has moved the focus of the debate off of Erasmus's original definition of free choice or a free will. For Erasmus, the free will is an innate ability to decide either to do one thing or another. In his case, he believes that one must do what is right given the opportunity. For Luther, the idea of a "free will" is a fiction. Instead, the entire orientation of our human nature after the Fall has turned against God. It is bound to sin. A person can still decide trivial matters of day-to-day life. One can decide to wear brown pants or blue ones. One can even decide to do a good deed but doing a good deed does not fulfill God's law and therefore they fall short of glory of God. As such we remain bound in our sinful state. To Erasmus, this made man an automaton dependent upon God.

Luther acknowledges the difficulty of what he says. It confounds our reason. It seems on some level to be unjust. Luther, however, said that when we confront such a difficulty we must remember that God is God and we are not. We must let God be God and trust in him.[18] He has declared that "while we were yet sinners, Christ died for us" (Rom. 5.8). It is difficult to trust God, but Luther urges us to do so. "For if you doubt or disdain to know that God foreknows all things, not contingently, but necessarily and immutably, how can you believe his promises and place a sure trust and reliance on them? For when he promises anything, you ought to be certain that he knows and is able and willing to perform what he promises; otherwise, you will regard him as neither truthful nor faithful and that is an impiety and a denial of the Most High God."[19]

How does one, then, come to be in a position to trust in God's promises? To answer this question, Luther turns to the distinction between the Law and the Gospel. For Erasmus, the law demonstrates for us how we ought to live so that we might be saved. For Luther, it plays a much different role in a person's life. It is a gift from God that destroys our naïve self-deception in our own ability to save ourselves. "It is the task, function, and effect of the law to be a light to the ignorant and blind, but such a light as reveals sickness, sin, death, hell, the wrath of God, though it affords no help and brings no deliverance from these, but is content to have revealed them. Then when a man becomes aware of the disease of sin, he is troubled, distressed, even in despair. The law is no help."[20] For Luther, following the law cannot save us because that is not the role of law. The law shows us how helpless we truly are. Fortunately, according to Luther, we are not abandoned in this despair. God offers a remedy to people

---

18 Luther writes, "I think it is sufficiently shown by these words that it is not permissible for men to pry into the will of Divine Majesty." Rupp and Watson, eds., *Luther and Erasmus: Free Will and Salvation*, 207.
19 Ibid., 122.
20 Ibid., 305–6.

caught in sin, "This is the voice of the gospel, revealing Christ as the deliverer."[21]

A significant portion of the debate between Luther and Erasmus focused on the implications of Luther's belief that we must simply trust in God's promise that he will save us. They debated questions of predestination, election, and the distinction between God's foreknowledge of who shall be saved and God's preordaining those who shall be saved. While Luther engaged in this discussion, it was not centrally important to his self-understood role as a preacher. In his preaching, he rarely discussed any of those topics, choosing instead to focus, again, on what God promises.

---

21 Ibid., 306.

CHAPTER 6

THE ANTICHRIST

Many Europeans in the sixteenth century believed that they were living in the last days of creation. The advancement of Muslim Turkish armies out of the Balkans and into Central Europe seemed to portend the end of days. Martin Luther also believed that the final judgment of God was nearing. A large part of Luther's understanding of the apocalypse and the last days focused on his belief that the papacy was controlled by the Antichrist. How did Luther come to this opinion? In this chapter, we will explore a number of events that happened in 1520 that convinced Luther that the Antichrist was at work in the world seeking to destroy creation.

While earlier in his career Luther viewed the Antichrist as a figure to come in the future, in 1520 Luther came to view the pope and the papacy as the Antichrist. Luther's view of the Antichrist and of the papacy shifted suddenly, dramatically, and permanently. There are a number of possible explanations for this shift in his view. First, the Indulgence Controversy was now at full boil and he faced an increasingly tenuous position legally and ecclesiastically. Second, he had appeared recently in Augsburg before Cardinal Cajetan and that meeting had gone spectacularly badly. A leading view is that he knew that Pope Leo X was preparing to ban and then excommunicate him. All of these certainly played a role, but the deciding factor was actually a short humanist tract against a medieval papal document. In 1520, Luther received a copy of Lorenzo Valla's *Discourse on the Forgery of the Alleged Donation of Constantine*.

THE SO-CALLED *DONATION OF CONSTANTINE*

The *Donation of Constantine* has been called the "best-known forgery in history."[1] This is, perhaps, an overstatement. It is not an overstatement, however, to say that it was one of the best-known documents in the medieval era and that Valla's *Discourse*, although not the first to challenge the authenticity of the document, is one of the greatest examples of Renaissance scholarship.[2] The *Donation of Constantine* records the Emperor Constantine's gift of the Western Empire, the lands of Italy, and the primacy over other patriarchal sees to Sylvester, bishop of Rome, in 314 or 315. Lorenzo Valla wrote the *Discourse on the Forgery of the Alleged Donation of Constantine* in 1440 while secretary to Alphonso, king of Aragon, Sicily, and Naples, as a part of Alphonso's attempts to delegitimize the papacy's claim to Sicily and Naples. It remained in manuscript form until published by Ulrich von Hutten in 1519.[3] It begins with a short introduction that lays out the argument that the document is a forgery. Following the introduction, Valla turns to show that Constantine was not the type of emperor to give away his empire and Pope Sylvester was not the type of churchman to accept it.[4]

Luther already knew that the *Donation of Constantine* had been used by medieval popes to justify their spiritual and secular preeminence over emperors and kings. What he did not know until he read Valla was that it was forged in order to steal the empire from "all [the] kings and princes of the West" to whom it rightfully belonged.[5] It was then fraudulently and with malice aforethought inserted into medieval law books in order to lend it authority.[6] Up to this point in

---

1 Cantor, 176. Cantor, of course, is not the only person to make this claim. There are literally hundreds of similar claims made about the *Donation*.

2 See Backus, 2003, 36–39.

3 Valla, 1519. A short publication run was done in 1517, then the more extensive run in 1519. It was later incorporated into *Opera* editions of Valla's works. See Valla, 1922, 3.

4 For Constantine, see Valla, 1922, 30–47; for Sylvester, 49–62.

5 Valla, 1922, 27.

6 "And first, not only must I convict of dishonesty him who tried to play Gratian and added sections to the work of Gratian, but also must convict of ignorance those who think a copy of the deed of gift is contained in Gratian; for the well-informed have never thought so, nor is it found in

his career, Luther had been growing increasingly uncomfortable with the idea that the pope had secular powers and authority; that growing feeling now found confirmation and validation. After reading Valla, Luther wrote:

> Therefore let every Christian believe that in these passages Christ does not give either to St. Peter or to the other Apostles the power to rule, or to soar so high. What then does He give? I will tell you. These words of Christ are nothing but gracious promises, given to the whole Church . . . When these comforting words of Christ, given for the benefit of all poor consciences in the whole Church, are thus made to strengthen and establish papal power, I will tell you of what it reminds me. It reminds me of a rich, kind prince who threw open his treasure-house, and gave complete freedom to all the poor to come and take what they needed. Among the needy there came a rogue, who made use of the permission all by himself and allowed none to come in who did not bow completely to his will, and arbitrarily explained the words of the prince to mean that the permission was given to him alone. Can you imagine what the kind prince would think of this rogue?[7]

---

any of the oldest copies of the Decretum. And if Gratian had mentioned it anywhere, he would have done so, not where they put it, breaking the thread of the narrative, but where he treats of the agreement of Louis [the Pious]. Besides, there are two thousand passages in the Decretum which forbid the acceptance of this passage; for example, that where the words of Melchiades, which I have cited above, are given. Some say that he who added this chapter [the Donation of Constantine] was called Palea, either because that was his real name or because what he added of his own, compared with Gratian, is as straw [palea] beside grain. However that may be, it is monstrous to believe that the compiler of the Decretum either did not know what was interpolated by this man, or esteemed it highly and held it for genuine. Good! It is enough! We have won! First, because Gratian does not say what they lyingly quote; and more especially because on the contrary, as can be seen in innumerable passages, he denies and disproves it; and last, because they bring forward only a single unknown individual, of not the least authority, so very stupid as to affix to Gratian what cannot be harmonized with his other statements." Valla, 1922, 75.

7 *On the Papacy at Rome* (1520), in *PE* 1: 378; *WA* 6: 312. Luther uses the word *schalckhafftiger* to describe the rogue. He uses this same adjective to describe the devil as well. For example, see *WA* 32: 491. Luther read Valla

It was the insight into the papacy's desire to control all the world, when combined with the neglect of its proper spiritual role, that helped confirm for Martin Luther that he faced not simply a corrupt and corrupting institution, but the very Antichrist itself.[8]

THE ANTICHRIST

The word Antichrist appears in the New Testament only five times; each time in the Johannine epistles (1 John 2.18 [twice], 2.22, 4.3; 2 John 7). None of these, however, played a significant role in Christian thinking regarding the Antichrist and the apocalypse. Instead, 2 Thessalonians became the *locus classicus*.[9] In 2 Thessalonians 2.1–12, Paul describes an eschatological battle between good and evil that was quickly linked with the image of the Antichrist.[10] Paul uses two terms for the Antichrist and highlights events that will precede or accompany the advent of the Antichrist. The first term Paul uses for the Antichrist is "the Man of Sin."[11] The second is "the Son of

---

in February and wrote *On the Papacy* in early May, for a full chronology, see Hendrix, 95–6.

8 These two aspects of the papacy (avarice and negligence) are nicely summed up by Valla in the conclusion to the *Discourse*, "The Pope both thirsts for the goods of others and drinks up his own: he is what Achilles calls Agamemnon, 'a people-devouring king.' The Pope not only enriches himself at the expense of the republic, as neither Verres nor Catiline nor any other embezzler dared to do, but he enriches himself at the expense of even the church and the Holy Spirit as old Simon Magus himself would abhor doing. And when he is reminded of this and is reproved by good people occasionally, he does not deny it, but openly admits it, and boasts that he is free to wrest from its occupants by any means whatever the patrimony given the church by Constantine; as though when it was recovered Christianity would be in an ideal state,-and not rather the more oppressed by all kinds of crimes, extravagances and lusts; if indeed it can be oppressed more, and if there is any crime yet uncommitted!" Valla, 1922, 179.

9 Pelikan, 74.

10 Chrysostom, I: 13: 386: "Paul discusses the Antichrist . . . but calls him the 'son of perdition' because he will be destroyed . . . He will abolish all the gods and will order men to worship him instead of God."

11 2 Thessalonians 2.3. *Nouum Testamentum*, 1550, Giiii^r. There is a textual variant to this text, ὁ ἄνθρωπος τῆς ἀνομίας "the Man of Lawlessness." Though this reading has since been determined to be the more authoritative, in the sixteenth and seventeenth centuries, the Man of Sin was considered

Perdition."[12] The Man of Sin and Son of Perdition will overthrow worship and demand to be worshiped. He will declare himself God. He will ultimately, though, be revealed (*apokalupthasetai*—this is where we get the word apocalypse) and destroyed when Christ comes again.[13]

Theologians in the medieval era focused more of their attention on the events that would accompany the apocalypse than they spent discerning the identity of the Man of Sin. Blasphemy, the persecution of true believers, the usurpation of God's rightful worship, and the fomenting of lawlessness were all lifted up as signs that the Antichrist was initiating the apocalypse.[14] Pope Gregory the Great (540–604; r. 590), for example, saw the military advancement of the Lombards as evidence that the Antichrist was at work in the world. Gregory internalized the Antichrist and argued that in light of the Lombards, each Christian must become aware of the Antichrist within.[15] When attention did turn to identifying the Man of Sin he was variously identified as the emperor, heretical leaders, Mohammed, or a leader of the Jews.[16]

One of the earliest identifications of the papacy with the Antichrist arose during the eleventh century during the conflict between Pope Gregory VIII (Hildebrand c. 1021–1085; r. 1073) and Holy Roman Emperor Henry IV (1050–1106; r. 1056/1065). Both men believed that the other was either the Antichrist or in league with him. For example, Cardinal Beno, a supporter of Henry, wrote that "Hildebrand is either a member of Antichrist, or Antichrist himself."[17] Joachim of Fiore (c. 1132–1202) was the era's most prolific writer on the Antichrist and comes very close to identifying the papacy with the Antichrist when he wrote in his *Expositio in Apocalypsim*:

> Just as the Beast from the Sea is held to be a great king from his sect who is like Nero and almost emperor of the whole world, so the Beast ascending from earth is held to be a great prelate who

authoritative. Stephanus's 1550 *Novum Testamentum* is one of the most important editions of Erasmus's Greek New Testament because it is the first early modern Greek New Testament to incorporate a critical textual apparatus. He has the variant in a marginal note and connects it to manuscripts.

12 2 Thessalonians 2.3, *Nouum Testamentum*, 1550, Giiii[r].
13 2 Thessalonians 2.8, *Nouum Testamentum*, 1550, Giiii[r].
14 See Emmerson, 83–95.
15 See McGinn, 81.
16 For example, Procopius used Antichrist motifs to describe Justinian in the seventh century. See McGinn, 83–84.
17 Beno, *The Deeds of the Roman Church against Hildebrand*. McGinn, 121.

will be like Simon Magnus and like a universal pope in the entire world. He is that Antichrist of whom Paul said he would be lifted up and opposed to everything that is said to be God, or that is worshipped, and that he would sit in God's temple showing himself as God [2 Thess. 2.4][18]

The identification of the papacy with the Antichrist continued to develop as the medieval era progressed. By the sixteenth century, a rough outline of the Antichrist's activity can be identified. Accordingly, the Antichrist will (1) betray the church from within, (2) undermine the Roman Empire, and (3) take God's rightful place in the Church and mislead through false doctrines and signs. As Luther looked about him in 1520, he believed only one figure in history fulfilled all these requirements—the pope.

LUTHER AND THE PAPAL ANTICHRIST

Among the many wars that Luther did not intend to start in 1517, the one with the papacy certainly takes pride of place. Reflecting on his own opinion of the papacy in 1517, Luther writes in 1545, "I was once a monk and a most enthusiastic papist when I began the cause."[19] He was also shocked by how quickly the debate with Teztel, Eck, and Prierias turned from a debate on the theological merits of indulgences to a debate on the actual authority of the pope; by his meeting in October 1518 with Cardinal Cajetan, the entire debate centered on papal authority. Despite Luther's best efforts to move the discussion back to theology, Cajetan would not move. For Cajetan (like Eck and Prierias) papal authority was a theological issue.[20] The November 1518 papal bull (authored by Cajetan following his meeting with Luther) *Cum postquam* is framed around indulgences and papal authority.

The meeting with Cajetan and the bull seem to be a turning point for Luther regarding the identification of the pope with the Antichrist. In a private letter to Wenceslaus Link (11 December 1518), Luther first reveals a nagging question of whether or not "the true

18 Joachim of Fiore, *Expositio*, 168ʳ, quoted in McGinn, 141–2.
19 "Preface to the Complete Edition of Luther's Latin Writings," *LW* 34: 328; *WA* 54: 179.
20 Carter Lindberg has persuasively argued that Luther's understanding of papal authority was clarified by Prierias and that Prierias played a significant role in Luther's developing thought regarding the papal Antichrist. See Lindberg, 1972.

Antichrist according to Paul is reigning in the Roman curia."[21] As he prepared for the debate at Leipzig, Luther expressed similar misgivings to George Spalatin, "And, confidentially, I do not know whetherthe pope is the Antichrist himself or whether he is his apostle, so miserably is Christ (that is, the truth) corrupted and crucified by the pope in the decretals."[22] What becomes obvious is that during this time period Luther was beginning to believe that the pope's policies and decretals were fundamentally anti-Christian. He had also become convinced that the papacy was tyrannical. What he was not yet convinced of was whether the pope was *the* Antichrist. The Leipzig Disputation would help him clarify this point.

The Leipzig Disputation is important for two reasons. First, Luther was forced by Johannes Eck to acknowledge that some of what he was arguing was similar to if not identical to the positions held by Jan Hus. This charge had first been leveled at Luther by Tetzel in early 1518.[23] When Luther declared that Hus was "Christian and evangelical," it clearly put him at odds with the papacy in a concrete and verifiable way. In late 1519, Luther would begin to read Hus in earnest. He was shocked by how much he did hold in common with the condemned heretic. In mid-February 1520, Luther revealed this surprise in a private letter to Spalatin, "I have taught and held all the teachings of John Hus, but thus far did not know it. John Staupitz has taught it in the same unintentional way. In short we all are Hussites and did not know it. Even Paul and Augustine are in reality Hussites. See the monstrous things into which we fall, I ask you, even without the Bohemian leader and teacher. I am so shocked that I do not know what to think when I see such terrible judgments of God over mankind, namely, that the most evident evangelical truth was burned in public and was already considered condemned more than one hundred years ago."[24] Second, as a result of the debate and his reading of Hus, Luther was forced to begin to discern what a godly papacy would look like.[25] When he compared his positive list to Leo X and many of his predecessors, he found them lacking.

---

21 *WABR* 1: 270.

22 *LW* 48: 111; *WABR* 2: 48–9.

23 See Grane, 21.

24 *LW* 48: 151; *WABR* 2: 41–2.

25 Hendrix, 93. Hus does contain a description of fours signs for an erring pope. Though a pope who stubbornly persisted in these errors could be considered the Antichrist, Hus never claimed that the pope was the Antichrist. For a discussion of Hus, see Leff, 662–707.

Thus, in early February 1520, Luther found the pope severely wanting, he was tyrannical, he was anti-Christian; but Luther was not yet convinced he was the Antichrist.[26] Most interpreters of Luther's stance regarding the papacy see the weight of the events of 1519 and the impending excommunication in 1520 as the reasons for Luther's new-found clarity. However, Luther actually had some cause for optimism in late 1519 and early 1520 rather than a pessimism that would have led him to see the pope as the Antichrist. On 12 January 1519, Emperor Maximilian I died. Luther's prince now stepped into the role of imperial caretaker until the next emperor was elected. On 28 June 1519, Charles V was elected to replace his grandfather. This was a positive development for Luther on a number of fronts. First, Charles's election promises assured that Luther would be given a hearing in Germany rather than Rome.[27] Second, Charles was a very well-educated prince with distinct humanist appreciations. For example, Charles was a lifelong supporter of his former tutor Erasmus and in 1519 Luther and Erasmus were still writing positive things about each other.[28] Third, Charles had a personal affection for Frederick the Wise. Fourth, Charles was not, nor would he ever really become, an ally of the pope.[29] He had his own dynastic reasons to stymie the pope. All these factors would have led Luther to see 1520 as a time of possibility rather than impending doom. An example of Luther's hopes regarding Charles can be found in a letter he wrote to the emperor on 30 August 1520

---

26 See Preuss, 111–14.
27 *DR* I: 865–76. English translation in Hillerbrand, 87: "We will also see to it and in no way allow that henceforth anybody, or high or low estate, elector, ruler, or otherwise, is without cause and without having been heard declared an outlaw. In all such cases a regular proceeding according to the statutes of the Holy Roman Empire is to be held and administered."
28 This positive estimation continued into 1520. For example, in November 1520, while the imperial court met in Cologne, Erasmus met with Frederick the Wise. This meeting led to the publication of *Axiomata Erasmi Roterodami pro causa Martini Lutheri.*
29 For example, the papacy sought the election of Francis, I of France over Charles. In early 1519, the curia reversed its earlier position demanding the immediate arrest and transport of Luther to Rome. In an attempt to swing Frederick to their side, they dispatched an envoy with a famous gold rose and a modified response to Luther. Rather than arrest, he would meet with the papal envoy in Augsburg. The original letter to Cardinal Cajetan demanding Luther's arrest (23 August 1518) and the revised letter of 11 September 1518 are discussed in *WA* 2: 23–5; *LW* 31: 286–9.

requesting a hearing of his case. This is not a naïve letter, nor dishonest fawning. Luther genuinely believed that Charles would grant him a fair and open hearing. He also believed if he got such a hearing, he would prevail.[30] Thus, the events of 1519 and even the possibility of a papal ban cannot alone account for Luther's change of opinion. One piece to the puzzle was still missing; this would come when he read Lorenzo Valla.

In late 1519, Ulrich von Hutten published his second edition of Valla's *Discourse*. A copy of Hutten's edition was given to Luther in early 1520 and he began to read it in February.[31]

As we have already noted, Valla helped convince Luther that papal claims to secular authority were unfounded. Further, the attempts by the papacy to secure those claims through treachery and deceit proved that the pope sought to overthrow the emperor and rule in his stead. After reading Valla, Luther again wrote to Spalatin. In the letter he refers specifically to Valla's treatise and all the earlier equivocation regarding the papal Antichrist is absent: "I have here at my disposal Hutten's edition of Lorenzo Valla's *Confutation of the Donation of Constantine* . . . I am greatly tormented, I do not even doubt that the pope is properly the Antichrist, that even the whole world's popular opinion expects; everything which he does, lives, speaks, and declares fit perfectly."[32]

---

30 "I come, helpless and poor; as the most worthless of men, I am prostrate before the feet of Your Most Serene Majesty, yet I bring forward a most worthy cause . . . I am now for the third year enduring limitless provocations, insults, perils, and whatever evil the wicked can devise. In the meantime I vainly offer silence, I vainly suggest conditions for peace, I vainly request to be informed of teachings more correct than mine. There is only one thing prepared for me: to be annihilated, together with the whole gospel. I have vainly tried everything. Therefore it has finally seemed wise to appeal to [Your] Imperial Majesty, according to the example of St. Athanasius, in case the Lord deigns to help his cause through [Your Imperial Majesty]. Humbly and on my knees, therefore, I beseech Your Most Serene Majesty, Charles, foremost of kings on earth, to deign to take under the shadow of your wings not me but this very cause of truth, since it is only by this truth that authority is given you to carry the sword for the punishment of the evil and for the praise of the good." "Letter to Emperor Charles V (30 August 1520)" *LW* 48: 177; *WABR* 2: 175–6.

31 Hendrix, 98.

32 *WABR* 2: 48: I have abbreviated the quote in translation. The full quote reads, "*Habeo in manibus officio Dominici Schleupner Donationem*

Luther would never again return to his hesitant position. Soon afterward he would respond to the taunts of the pro-papal Franciscan Augustine von Alveld with the pamphlet *On the Papacy at Rome: Against the Most Celebrated Romanist in Leipzig*. He began work on the document in early May 1520 and it was published on 26 June.[33] He would not read the papal bull banning him for another five months.[34] And yet, the change of position is already apparent here. Luther writes,

Why then does the Roman see so furiously desire the whole world? Why did it steal and rob country, city, indeed, principalities and

---

Constantini A Laurentio Vallensi confutatam per Huttenum editam. Deus bone, quantę seu tenebrę seu nequitię Romanensium & quod in Dei iuditio mireris per tot sęcula non modo durasse, Sed etiam preualuisse ac inter decretales relata esse. tam Impura tam crassa tam impudentia mendacia inque fidei articulorum (nequid monstrosissimi monstri desit) vicem successisse. Ego sic angor, vt prope non dubitem papam esse proprie Antichristum illum, quem vulgata opinione expectat mundus; adeo conueniunt omnia, quae viuit, facit, loquitur, statuit."

33 *WA* 6: 280. During this same time, Luther would also publish a forward to Sylvester Prierias's anti-Luther tract, *Epitoma responsionis ad Martinum Luther*. Where earlier responses to Prierias attacked his reasoning and his distortions of Luther's writings, now in this preface, Luther connects Prierias's understanding of papal power with the papal Antichrist (the word *Antichrist* does not appear in any of the previous writings between Prierias and Luther), "If one so thinks and writes [about the pope] in Rome, with the knowledge of the pope and cardinals (which I hope is not so), then I freely declare with this writing that the true Antichrist sits in the temple of God and rules his Babel, is clothed in purple in Rome and that the Roman court is the school of Satan . . . Who is the Antichrist, if such a pope is not the Antichrist? (*Quid est Antichristus, si talis Papa non est Antichristus*)" *WA* 6: 328, quoted in Lindberg, 1972, 61, translation altered.

34 Luther received the bull, *Exsurge Domine* on 10 October 1520. His responses to the banning continue the Antichrist polemic. He began work on the first, *Adversus execrabilem Antichristi bullam*, on 4 November 1520. It was published on 1 December. *WA* 6: 595–612; here 602: "*Nonne tu es homo ille peccati et filius perditionis, qui negat deum, emptorem suum, et charitatem veritatis tollit, ut operationem erroris sui statuat, quo credamus iniquitati, ut Paulus praedixit? Si enim articulus haereticus non est, non potest esse offensivus aut scandalosus nisi haereticis Antichristis et Satanis pietatis.*" Luther expanded this tract and translated it into German later in the month, *Widder die Bullen des Antichrists* (*WA* 6: 614–29).

kingdoms, and now dares to produce, ordain, dismiss, and change as it pleases all kings and princes, as if it were the Antichrist? Where is the figure fulfilled here?[35]

In this denunciation, we also hear an echo of Valla. We have already noted Valla's contention that the papacy sought the "whole West." The similarity between Luther and Valla on this point is more striking when one sees Valla's full text. "They say the city of Rome is theirs, theirs the kingdom of Sicily and of Naples, the whole of Italy, the Gauls, the Spains, the Germans, the Britons, indeed the whole West; for all these are contained in the instrument of the Donation itself. So all these are yours, supreme pontiff? And it is your purpose to recover them all? To despoil all kings and princes of the West of their cities or compel them to pay you a yearly tribute, is that your plan?"[36]

Luther's quotation above comes in the middle of a long discussion about the duties and responsibilities of Aaron and the high-priests of the Old Testament. Likewise, Valla contains a discussion on the role of the chief priests in ancient Israel. Using the first chief priest as his example Valla sardonically asks, "Did Aaron and others of the tribe of Levi take care of anything except the tabernacle of the Lord?"[37] Luther seems to have such a question in mind when he writes,

Again, in the Old Testament the high priest was not allowed to own any part of the land of Israel, but instead lived just from the contributions of the people of Israel . . . The old high priest was a subject ruled by kings. Why then does the pope allow his feet to be kissed, and why does he want to be king of all kings—something even Christ himself did not do?[38]

---

35 *On the Papacy in Rome: Against the Most Celebrated Romanist in Leipzig* (May 1520), *LW* 39: 84; *WA* 6: 308, translation altered.
36 Valla, 1922, 27.
37 Ibid., 53.
38 *On the Papacy in Rome* (May 1520), *LW* 39: 84; *WA* 6: 308, translation altered.

He would continue this line of argument in the later treatises of 1520, *On the Babylonian Captivity*,[39] *To the Christian Nobility*,[40] and *The Freedom of a Christian*.[41]

THE EFFECTS OF LUTHER'S VIEW

Luther's belief that Pope Leo X represented the Antichrist and was waging a war not to destroy him but to undermine the very fabric of

---

39 *WA* 6: 537; *LW* 36: 72: "Unless they will abolish their laws and ordinances, and restore to Christ's churches their liberty and have it taught among them, they are guilty of all the souls that perish under this miserable captivity, and the papacy is truly the kingdom of Babylon and of the very Antichrist. For who is "the man of sin" and "the son of perdition" [2 Thess. 2.3] but he who with his doctrines and his laws increases the sins and perdition of souls in the church, while sitting in the church as if he were God? [2 Thess. 2.4]. All this the papal tyranny has fulfilled, and more than fulfilled, these many centuries. It has extinguished faith, obscured the sacraments and oppressed the gospel; but its own laws, which are not only impious and sacrilegious, but even barbarous and foolish, it has decreed and multiplied without end."

40 *WA* 6: 429; *LW* 44: 193: "If there were no other base trickery to prove that the pope is the true Antichrist, this one would be enough to prove it. Hear this, O pope, not of all men the holiest but of all men the most sinful! O that God from heaven would soon destroy your throne and sink it in the abyss of hell! Who has given you authority to exalt yourself above your God, to break and loose his commandments, and teach Christians, especially the German nation, praised throughout history for its nobility, its constancy and fidelity, to be inconstant, perjurers, traitors, profligates, and faithless? God has commanded us to keep word and faith even with an enemy, but you have taken it upon yourself to loose his commandment and have ordained in your heretical, anti-Christian decretals that you have his power. Thus through your voice and pen the wicked Satan lies as he has never lied before. You force and twist the Scriptures to suit your fancy. O Christ, my Lord, look down; let the day of your judgment break clown and destroy this nest of devils at Rome. There sits the man of whom St. Paul said, "He shall exalt himself above you, sit in your church, and set himself up as God, that man of sin, the son of perdition" [2 Thess. 2.3–5]. What else is papal power but simply the teaching and increasing of sin and wickedness? Papal power serves only to lead souls into damnation in your name and, to all outward appearances, with your approval!"

41 *WA* 7: 49; *LW* 31: 375: "Unless faith is at the same time constantly taught, this happens easily and defiles a great many, as has been done until now through the pestilent, impious, soul-destroying traditions of our popes and the opinions of our theologians. By these snares numberless souls have been dragged down to hell, so that you might see in this the work of Antichrist."

the world's order had a number of almost immediate affects. First, it meant that if the pope followed through on the threat to excommunicate Luther that would be welcomed rather than dreaded. For Luther, it was a badge of honor to be condemned by the Antichrist. If he was so important to the Antichrist that he warranted the attention devoted to excommunication and the political maneuvering required to have him extradited to Rome for trial and execution, then it followed that the message that he was proclaiming was the Gospel and that the Gospel was a threat to the Antichrist. To be condemned by the Antichrist meant that he was truly representing Christ. When Luther finally received the papal bull threatening him with excommunication, he was given 90 days to recant. Instead of recanting, he went with a group of colleagues and students to the city wall and held a bonfire. Into the bonfire, the students and Luther threw the symbols of the Antichrist's reign—they burned the bull threatening him with execution, but they also burned a copy of the medieval church law books that contained the *Donation of Constantine*. Second, if the pope was the Antichrist then neither he nor those loyal to him could be expected to help reform the church. Since Luther could not count on church officials to help reform the church, he had to turn to others for help. As early as November 1517, he had written to Archbishop Albrecht of Mainz hoping that he would end indulgence sales for the sake of the souls entrusted to his care. Albrecht instead resisted him and was the first to begin church legal proceedings against him. Leo X and Albrecht would not help, but Frederick the Wise and other committed Christian leaders within the community might. Luther has been faulted at times for linking his reforms to secular authorities. One must ask, however, where else should he have turned? For Luther, the battle with the Antichrist was a battle over the souls of men and women. To set aside the fight meant that he was abandoning those souls to hell. When Luther turned to secular authorities to help him reform the decaying church, it was not because he thought that they were either the best people or the most appropriate people to reform the church. They were not. Rightfully, it should have been fellow clergy, but those clerical leaders above him were now, in his mind, bound to the Antichrist. He turned to the secular lords because there was nowhere else to turn. Finally, the view that the pope was the Antichrist gave Luther hope. Ironically, the power of the Antichrist would be greatest and it would react with the greatest ferocity when it was actually most threatened. The ends to which the papal court went to destroy Luther convinced him that the Antichrist was in its final death throws. Christ would return soon. Christ's return would mean a terrible judgment for the Antichrist and his minions, but it was a consolation to true and faithful Christians. At the end of his very long introduction to the book of Daniel in the Old Testament, Luther writes of this hope at the end times:

> This Daniel we commend to the reading of all good Christians, to whom he is comforting and useful in these wretched, last times . . . For the prophecies of Daniel, and others like them, are not written simply that men may know history and the tribulations that are to come, and thus satisfy their curiosity, as with a news report, but in order that the righteous shall be encouraged and made joyful, and strengthened in faith and hope and patience. For here the righteous see and hear that their misery shall have an end, that they are to be freed from sins, death, the devil, and all evil—a freedom for which they yearn—and be brought into heaven, to Christ, into his blessed, everlasting kingdom.[42]

---

42 *LW* 35: 294.

PART III

LUTHER'S SOCIAL AND POLITICAL ENGAGEMENTS

CHAPTER 7

POLITICS, AUTHORITY, AND JUST RESISTANCE

In 1996, the German historian and Luther scholar, Bernhard Lohse wondered if the Luther presented by some would recognize the Luther described by others.[1] When one turns to Luther's political theology, the task of trying to recognize the "real" Luther becomes especially difficult. Beginning in the sixteenth century, Luther's contemporaries portrayed him in absolutely contradictory roles. Thomas Müntzer accused Luther of being a "toady of princes" and called him "Father Pussyfoot," for being unwilling to join Müntzer's revolution. On the other hand, Johannes Cochlaeus accused Luther of fomenting Müntzer's revolt and uprising calling him the "cause of all evils, miseries, and calamities of this sort."[2] Both Müntzer and Cochlaeus viewed Luther negatively. Interestingly, Luther believed that his political theology was actually one of the most helpful discussions on the topic. In 1526, he noted with some irony that not everyone shared his high esteem of his work. He wrote that "not since the time of the apostles have the temporal sword and temporal authority been so clearly described or so highly praised as by me. Even my enemies must admit this, but the reward, honor, and thanks that I have earned by it are to have my doctrine called seditious and condemned as resistance to rulers."[3] The negative appraisal of Luther's theology has continued into the present era. In the nineteenth century, the church historian Ernst Troeltsch argued that Luther's political

---

1 Bernhard Lohse, *Martin Luther's Theology: Its Historical and Systematic Development*, trans. and ed. Roy A. Harrisville (Edinburgh: T & T Clark, 1999), 3–6.
2 *Luther's Lives*, 165.
3 *Whether Soldiers, too, Can be Saved*, *LW* 46: 95 (translation altered, compare *WA* 19: 625).

theology encouraged "quietism." By quietism, Troeltsch meant that Luther required his followers to quietly obey their secular rulers regardless of their actions. Troeltsch writes,

> Lutheran Christian individualism has retired behind the line of battle of all external events and outward activity, into a purely personal spirituality. This spirituality is based on nothing save the "Word," which is guaranteed by the Church: it therefore regards the Church simply as the Herald of the Word, endowed with a purely spiritual miraculous converting power; it has no conception of the Church as an ethical organization of Christendom as a whole. As soon as the Christian believer turns from this spirituality to take his part in real life, he can only express his inner liberty through submission to the existing order.[4]

Shortly after World War II, the journalist William Shirer took Troeltsch's assertion a step farther and argued that there was a direct connection between Lutheran theology and the rise of Adolf Hitler. In his discussion of the "Historical Roots of the Third Reich," he writes,

> Through his sermons and his magnificent translation of the Bible, Luther created the modern German language, aroused in the people not only a new Protestant vision of Christianity but a fervent nationalism and taught them, at least in religion, the supremacy of the individual conscience. But, tragically for them, Luther's siding with the princes in the peasant uprisings, which he had largely inspired, and his passion for political autocracy ensure a mindless and provincial political absolutism which reduced the vast majority of the German people to poverty, to a horrible torpor and a demeaning subservience.[5]

Whether criticizing Luther for being too supportive of the government or for encouraging revolution the one thing remains fairly constant

---

4 Ernst Troeltsch, *The Social Teaching of the Christian Churches*, trans. Oliver Wyon, 2 volumes (1931, reprint ed., New York: Harper & Row, 1960), 2: 540.

5 William L. Shirer, *The Rise and Fall of the Third Reich: A History of Nazi Germany* (New York: Simon & Schuster, 1960), 91.

across all critiques is the source of Luther's major political short-coming—his theology of the Two Kingdoms.[6]

TWO KINGDOMS

Since the very earliest days of Christianity, the church and its theologians have struggled with how to approach the relationship between a Christian and the government. Part of the confusion can be traced to the New Testament itself. In the synoptic Gospels, when Jesus was confronted by a group of Pharisees discussing the topic he told them to "render unto Caesar the things that are Caesar's and unto God the things that are God's."[7] Both Peter and Paul attempt to honor this charge but offer different opinions. Paul tells Christians in Romans 13 that they must be subject to authority for all secular authorities are ordained by God. Peter, however, disobeys a governmental command in Acts 5 and when questioned about his refusal to cease preaching the good news of Jesus' resurrection, he declares that it is better to serve God than man.

Luther sought to develop a theology of political engagement that honored Christ's command but did not fall into the either/or dichotomy of either complete submission or total resistance to governing authorities. He patterned his thought on Augustine. Augustine argued that Christians live in two cities; the earthly city of this world that is fleeting and temporary and the heavenly city of God that is a Christian's true home and is eternal. In the early 1520s, Luther expanded Augustine's concept of two cities into his own doctrine of the Two Kingdoms in two major treatises: *An Open Letter to the Christian Nobility of the German Nation Concerning the Reform of*

---

6 For a recent example of this see Alister E. McGrath, *Reformation Thought: An Introduction*, 2nd ed. (Cambridge, MA: Blackwell Publishers, 1993), 209–10: "Luther reinforced [the princes'] political authority by grounding it in divine providence. God governs the world, including the church, through the princes and magistrates. The church is in this world, and so must submit itself to the world order . . . The way was [thus] opened to the eventual domination of the church by the state, which was a virtual universal trait of Lutheranism. The failure of the German church to oppose Hitler in the 1930's is widely seen as reflecting the inadequacies of Luther's political thought."

7 Matthew 22.21; Mark 12.17; Luke 20.25.

the Christian Estate in 1520 and the 1523 treatise *On Temporal Authority: To What Extent Should It be Obeyed.*

Luther used two terms when speaking of the Two Kingdoms.[8] The first is the two realms (*Zwei Reiche*) because it refers to the two spheres of one's existence: before God and before humanity. The *geistliche Reich* (the spiritual realm) is one's existence before God. The *weltliche Reich* (the worldly realm) refers to one's existence in the human community. Here Luther has slightly altered Augustine.

---

8 I have chosen to continue using the phrase Two Kingdoms for two reasons. First, it is far better known and has far more literature devoted to it than do the more technically precise terms (Realm and Government), thus our discussion here can be more easily placed within that body of work. But, also, just as importantly, I believe the idea of the Two Kingdoms nicely apprehends the polyvalent nature of Luther's thought on the Two Realms and the Two Governments. If we allow ourselves to be too distracted by the technicalities of *Reich* verses *Regiment* we will fail to see the forest for the trees. The two ideas form a cooperative whole that can best be maintained by continuing to speak of Two Kingdoms. The literature on the Two Kingdoms is vast, some of the most important works on the subject include: Paul Althaus, *The Ethics of Martin Luther*, translated by Robert C. Schultz (Philadelphia: Fortress Press, 1972) and his "Luthers Lehre von den beiden Reichen im Feuer der Kritik," *Lutherjahrbuch* 24 (1957): 40–67; Heinrich Bornkamm, *Luther's Doctrine of the Two Kingdoms in the Context of His Theology (* Philadelphia: Fortress, 1966); Thomas Brady, "Luther and Society: Two Kingdoms or Three Estates? Tradition and Experience in Luther's Social Teaching," *Lutherjahrbuch* 52 (1985): 197–224; W. J. D. Cargill Thompson, *The Political Thought of Martin Luther* (New Jersey: Barnes & Noble Books, 1984) and his "The 'Two Kingdoms' and the 'Two Regiments': Some Problems of Luther's Zwei-Reiche-Lehre," *Journal of Theological Studies* 20 (1969): 164–85; Ulrich Duchrow and Wolfgang Huber, editors. *Die Ambivalenz der Zweireicheslehre in lutherischen Kirchen des 20. Jahrhunderts* (Gütersloh: Gütersloher Verlagshaus, 1976); Gerhard Ebeling, "The Necessity of the Doctrine of the Two Kingdoms," in *Word and Faith*, translated by James W. Leitch (Philadelphia: Fortress, 1963), 386–406. More recent examinations include, Robert J. Bast, "From Two Kingdoms to Two Tablets: The Ten Commandments and the Christian Magistrate," *Archiv für Reformationsgeschichte* 89 (1998): 79–95; William H. Lazareth, *Christians and Society: Luther, the Bible, and Social Ethics* (Minneapolis: Fortress, 2001); Karl-Heinz zur Mühlen, "Two Kingdoms," in *Oxford Encyclopedia of the Reformation*, edited by Hans J. Hillerbrand (New York: Oxford, 1996), 4: 184–8; and David M. Whitford, "Martin Luther's Political Encounters," in *The Cambridge Companion to Martin Luther*, edited by Donald McKim (Cambridge and New York: Cambridge, 2003), 178–92.

While Augustine certainly viewed the earthly city and the heavenly city as existing simultaneously and that a Christian was, to a certain degree, a participant in both cities, Luther stresses the simultaneity of the spiritual and worldly realms far more than Augustine. Just as a Christian is simultaneously saint and sinner, he is also a member of both the worldly and spiritual realm at the same time.

For Luther, the spiritual realm is eternal and everlasting; it is the realm the Gospel, revelation, and faith. It is seen most clearly in the church. The spiritual realm exists to offer the grace of God to all through preaching the Word of God. Two themes run through Luther's thought about the spiritual realm: freedom and equality. Since Christians are free from the fear of damnation, they are also free from empty acts of penance that are often directed toward relics or other equally "dead" rituals. Instead, a Christian can now, in the surety of salvation, work in the world not to earn his salvation but to help and encourage his neighbors. According to Luther, Christians are perfectly free from obligations so that they might serve others.[9] Revolutionary in this understanding is the revision of status. The spiritual realm is not governed hierarchically. In this realm all Christians are equal. Luther writes,

> All Christians are truly of the spiritual estate, and there is no difference among them except that of office. Paul says in 1 Corinthians 12 [.12–13] that we are all one body, yet every member has its own work by which it serves the others. This is because we have one baptism, one gospel, and one faith, and are all Christians alike; for baptism, gospel, and faith alone make us spiritual and a Christian people . . . it follows from this argument that there is no true, basic difference between laymen and priests, princes and bishops, between religious [i.e., those living in monasteries] and secular, except for the sake of office and work, but not for the sake of status.[10]

Since in baptism there is no longer Jew nor Greek, slave nor free, in the spiritual realm there are no distinctions of class or authority.

---

9 Luther, *The Freedom of a Christian* (1520), *LW* 31: 343: "A Christian is a perfectly free lord of all, subject to none. A Christian is perfectly dutiful servant of all, subject to all."

10 Luther, *To the Christian Nobility of the German Nation* (1520), *LW* 44: 127, 129.

As Jesus explained to his disciples in Matthew 20, in the spiritual kingdom service to others is definitive not status. The worldly realm is the spiritual realm's dialectical partner; it is the realm of reason and unbelief. Both the worldly and spiritual realms exist through God's regulation of creation, but they play different roles. The worldly realm orders the communal life—in the home, in the city, and in the state.

In the spiritual realm there are no distinctions of status but there are different works or jobs that need to be done. For example, not everyone is called to preach. Likewise, in the worldly realm, people are called to different jobs and works. Here, however, status does play a role. Emperors are called to far greater responsibility than ordinary men and therefore are of a higher status and deserve greater standing within the community. To explain how these work within the worldly and spiritual realms, Luther used another set of paired terms that are part of the Two Kingdoms and can best be understood as operating within the two realms. These are the two governments (*Zwei Regimente*). The first (*das geistliche Regiment*) is the spiritual government of the church exercised through the proclamation of the Word of God and proper administration of the sacraments. Here Luther has reorganized the medieval understanding of church or spiritual government which would have been organized hierarchically under the authority of the pope. For Luther, the spiritual realm's fidelity must always be to the Gospel and not to the church's hierarchy. The second (*das weltliche Regiment*) is the worldly government of emperors, rulers, and ruled, which is governed by law and enforced by coercion. The responsibility of the secular realm is to limit the effects of sin and malfeasance and thus to ensure that the unjust will not run rampant over the weak and downtrodden.[11]

Thus, Luther attempted in the 1520s to set a new course in the relationship between the church and the state. Instead of one being the subject of the other, they each have clearly defined roles and spheres of influence that ought to be kept distinct.[12] The wisdom of

---

11 *On Temporal Authority* (1523): "[God] has subjected [the wicked] to the sword so that, even though they would like to, they are unable to practice their wickedness, and if they do practice it they cannot do so without fear or with success and impunity" (*LW* 45: 91; *WA* 11: 251).

12 *On Temporal Authority* (1523): "For this reason one must carefully distinguish between these two governments. Both must be permitted to remain; the one to produce righteousness, the other to bring about external peace

this perspective is the fact that pastors would make poor rulers and princes poor pastors. They would fail because they have neither the training nor the perspective to do the other's task. For Luther, the issue ultimately is one of trust. One must trust God and God's order of creation. The church has been given a special and unique position in creation. It is called to proclaim the Gospel. It must trust God and the power of his word. When the church trusts God, and lives its life in the spiritual realm, it is free from responsibilities that do not belong to it—like baptizing a particular government (as when they crown a king). Coronations of kings and emperors are not the responsibility of the church. When it focuses on such things, its message becomes confused.[13]

Rulers, princes, and even town magistrates, likewise, ought to trust that they too have been given a gift by God. They have been given the power of the sword by God for the maintenance of order and justice. This is a high and worthy office with great responsibility. The prince or magistrate ought to devote himself to that and leave the proclamation of the Word to the church. Thus, for Luther, each kingdom is entrusted by God with a special responsibility. While the kingdoms are complementary in that they are part of God's ordering of creation generally, Luther believed that they must remain distinct. The question that must yet be addressed, however, is whether or not one can be a political agent and remain a Christian? And further, what are one's options as a Christian when either the state or the church oversteps its bounds?

---

and prevent evil deeds. Neither one is sufficient in the world without the other. No one can become righteous in the sight of God by means of the temporal government, without Christ's spiritual government. Christ's government does not extend over all men; rather, Christians are always a minority in the midst of non-Christians. Now where temporal government or law alone prevails, there sheer hypocrisy is inevitable, even though the commandments be God's very own. For without the Holy Spirit in the heart no one becomes truly righteous, no matter how fine the works he does. On the other hand, where the spiritual government alone prevails over land and people, there wickedness is given free rein and the door is open for all manner of rascality, for the world as a whole cannot receive or comprehend it" (*LW* 45: 92; *WA* 11: 252).

13 For Luther, another example of the confusion between realms was when church leaders began to seek the accoutrements of regal authority. The best example of this for Luther was the Papal Tiara.

MAGISTRATES AND SOLDIERS: CAN ONE
STILL BE A CHRISTIAN?

Luther was largely a situational rather than systematic theologian. He rarely wrote a theological treatise simply for the purpose of explaining a doctrine. In the Wittenberg circle of professors and theologians that task often fell to Philip Melanchthon who prepared such works for classroom instruction called the *Loci Communes* (the Common Places of Theology). In contrast, Luther was almost always responding to a question or situation. As he was working out his understanding of the relationship between the church and the secular estates, he was asked a number of times whether or not a Christian could be a soldier and whether or not a Christian could participate in government.

The entire premise of *To the Christian Nobility* is that Christians can and should play a role in the civil life of their community. However, they must govern according to laws, tradition, fairness, and reason, not according to biblical mandate. Luther viewed this as liberating, many then (and still today) found it confusing. For Luther, one did not have to be a Christian in order to be an excellent ruler. One only had to be wise. In fact, Luther states that rulers might even be godless and still do God's work by limiting evil. He says as much when he writes that God preserves even the kingdoms of the Tartars and the Turks.[14]

When Luther turned to the question of war and soldiers, he took very seriously the question of a seasoned soldier who came to Luther in July 1525, while in Wittenberg on official duty, with a troubled conscience. Assa von Kamm had been in many battles over his lifetime and had recently led the Saxon army during the Peasants' War. Now, however, he was plagued by the question of whether or not being a soldier was compatible with the Gospel. Could one truly be a soldier and still be welcomed into heaven? Luther wrote, *Whether Soldiers, Too, May be Saved* in 1526 when other soldiers and advisors asked him to put into print the private consolation he had given to Kamm.[15]

---

14 *WA* 27: 418: "One need not be Christian to be a secular ruler. It is not necessary for the emperor to be a Christian or for him to rule as a Christian. It is enough that he have reason. Thus, the Lord God preserves the kingdoms of the Tartars and the Turks."

15 It is unlikely that Kamm ever actually got to read Luther's treatise. The publication of the *Soldiers* was delayed until 1527. By that point,

Luther assured soldiers that their profession was not necessarily opposed to the call of the Gospel. Certainly war and soldiering can and was abused. Wars could be fought for greed and profit. But, he also recognized that creation is fallen and that evil men sometimes prey upon the weak and helpless. In those times, a soldier must rise up to defend the weak as he has the responsibility to defend.[16] Thus, like Augustine and many other theologians before him, he rules out the idea of offensive wars.[17] He also views all wars as unjust and evil. Nevertheless, he says that sometimes a soldier must say to himself, "My neighbor compels and forces me to fight, though I would rather avoid it." In such a case, Luther says to the soldier that the campaign that they are involved in can "be called not only war, but lawful self-defense, for we must distinguish between wars that someone begins because that is what he wants to do and does before anyone else attacks him, and those wars that are provoked when an attack is made by someone else. The first kind can be called wars of desire; the second, wars of necessity. The first kind are of the devil; God does not give good fortune to the man who wages that kind of war. The second kind are human disasters; God help in them!"[18]

Thus, being a magistrate or a soldier was not a Christian office. They were, however, vocations that Christians could fill with a clear conscience as long as they governed their actions according to reason and justice. Luther disagreed with some more radical reformers who believed that Christians did not need a secular government and could not participate in a secular government. On the whole, he judged such positions as wildly naïve in that they greatly underestimated the power and prevalence of sin. In a world still trapped by sin, magistrates, rulers, and soldiers, when they did their jobs correctly

---

Kamm was again representing Saxony, this time in the army of Charles V during his Italian campaign. He contracted a now unknown illness in Italy and died in 1528.

16 *LW* 46: 119: "Look at the real soldiers, those who have played the game of war. They are not quick to draw their sword, they are not contentious; they have no desire to fight. But when someone forces them to fight, watch out! They are not playing games."

17 *LW* 46: 118: "It is not right to start a war just because some silly lord has gotten the idea into his head. At the very outset I want to say that whoever starts a war is in the wrong."

18 *LW* 46: 121.

and not selfishly, helped create a protective space in which people could work, live, and raise families.

Here Luther is making a fundamental distinction that he will continue to make whenever he wrote on politics or war or government. There is a fundamental distinction between the office and the person who holds the office. Governing authority, whether it be a great emperor or a humble town mayor, are given by God for the ordering of creation, the preservation of peace, and thriving of human community. The office, therefore, is always a good gift of God. Human beings, however, are sinful and thus the person filling an office can, and often did, misuse the office. He deals with such a question when he answered Kamm's concern about what one must do when a superior military official orders one to do something as a soldier that one knows is without question forbidden by God.

> A second question, "Suppose my lord were wrong to go to war?" I reply, If you know for sure that he is wrong, then you should fear God rather than men and you should neither fight nor serve, for you cannot have a good conscience before God.[19]

Luther here puts a significant restraint upon the soldier. Earlier in the text he notes that all overlords (even the emperor) become simply men when compared to God. God, therefore, must ultimately be served before any man (here Luther is alluding to Peter's declaration in Acts 5.29 that one must serve God and not man). This becomes very important when the overlord oversteps the boundaries of his office and seeks to do something which is forbidden by God. If, for example, God has ordained the soldier to defend the weak, then when a superior orders one to make war upon a neighbor that has not made war against you that is forbidden. If a soldier did participate in a war of aggression then that soldier had, indeed, put his salvation in jeopardy. In this case, the soldier responds by saying that he will be stripped of his authority, deprived of his land, and subjected to humiliation by the overlord who commands him to make war on the innocent. Luther realizes the cost that will be borne by such a soldier but nevertheless states, "You must take that risk and, with God's help let whatever happens, happen . . . In every other occupation we are also exposed to the danger that rulers will compel

---

19 *LW* 46: 130.

us to act wrongly; but since God will have us leave even father and mother for his sake, we must certainly leave lords for his sake."[20] What happened, however, when the governing authorities not only punished the soldier but turned on their own people in corruption and tyranny? In such a case leaving the lord was not possible. Was it possible, according to Luther, to resist such a tyrant?

LUTHER AND RESISTANCE TO TYRANNY

Luther's most significant treatise on the right to resist a tyrant was written following the 1530 Diet of Augsburg. In 1529, the imperial diet met in the small city of Speyer, which is about 20 miles southeast of Heidelberg. The meeting was held in March and one of the agenda items was religious innovation (which was a circumlocution for talking about Luther) within the empire. On 15 March, Charles V's younger brother Ferdinand, who as "King of the Romans" was filling in for him as chair of the diet, called for a vote that would outlaw religious innovation. He did not allow debate and with swift action, the vote was passed. The "evangelical" (or what would become "Lutheran") princes were stunned. They felt that holding a vote without allowing for discussion and debate was a violation of the empire's rules and laws. They drafted a *protestatio* (or a formal protest) that functioned as an appeal of the king's actions. It is from that document that we have the word "Protestant."[21] The king rejected their protest and sought to outlaw Lutheran theology and practice. The *Protestatio* is important historically because it outlines the main contours of the debate between the evangelical estates and the emperor. Most importantly, it argues that the emperor and the imperial diet did not have the authority to issue legislate matters of faith. Issues of religion were to be governed by the conscience and determined by a general church council. The "Protestants" pledged to obey the emperor in all things to which he was rightfully due; but in matters of faith, they would heed the advice offered by Luther to

---

20 *LW* 46: 130–1.
21 The "Protestants" included Duke John of Saxony, Margrave George of Brandenburg-Ansbach, the dukes Ernst and Franz of Braunschweig-Lüneburg, Landgrave Philipp of Hesse, Prince Wolfgang of Anhalt, and the cities of Strasbourg, Nuremberg, Ulm, Constance, Lindau, Memmingen, Kempten, Nördlingen, Heilbronn, Reutlingen, Isny, St. Gall, Weissenburg, and Windsheim.

Kamm and follow St. Peter by serving God before man. Even though Ferdinand did not originally accept the *Protestatio* it was a formal part of imperial legislative rules and so gave the Protestants some official standing and prevented the harshest aspects of outlawing Lutheranism.

After first attempting to ignore the implications of Speyer, Charles was finally forced to recognize that something had to be done to fix what Speyer had left before the empire. On 21 January 1530, he summoned an imperial diet to meet in Augsburg on 8 April. The official reason given for calling the diet was that the Ottoman Turks were again making border incursions into the empire and had to be stopped. Nevertheless, to Charles, the Ottoman threat and religious discord within the empire were tightly bound together. Religious discord and internal political fraction were not the foundations upon which he could hope to lay a successful campaign against the "invading infidel." The designation of the Turkish threat and the desire for unity as the central concerns of the diet was a brilliant political and tactical move on the part of the emperor because it placed the evangelical princes in a particularly difficult situation. They did not wish to be perceived as undermining the unity of the empire in the face of the "enemy," but they were also unwilling to abandon their religious convictions. In the medieval world, religious unity defined a healthy community. The Protestants began to argue something that to many of their peers seemed absurd on its face but today is accepted as fact: religious diversity did not undermine loyalty to the empire.

To support this new position, Saxony's emeritus chancellor, Gregor Brück,[22] recommended that the Protestants draw up a short justification of their theological and ecclesiastical reforms for the emperor. Their memorandum, which has been called the Torgau Articles since the nineteenth century, goes to great lengths (Article 1) to assert that the reforms of the evangelicals had not undermined the unity of the church and therefore had not eroded the unity of the empire.[23] This short defense of evangelical reforms was quickly abandoned

---

22 Brück (1484–1557) leadership in this work was immensely important to its success. He was widely respected for his legal mind and political acumen. He was also a stanch supporter of Luther.

23 Article 1, "On Human and Divine Ordinances," *The Torgau Articles*, translated by William R. Russell, in *Concord Sources*, 94–8.

once the evangelical delegation arrived in Augsburg and realized that a more detailed document would be needed. The resultant *Augsburg Confession* also went to great lengths to stress the unity of the Church (Articles 7 and 8) and the duty of Christians to serve the "public order and secular government" (Article 16).[24]

Despite the evangelicals' efforts to assure the emperor of their allegiance to the empire and the orthodoxy of their reforms, Charles remained unconvinced. Then the Catholic estates responded to the Protestants with their own *Confutation of the Augsburg Confession.*[25] The emperor liked the rebuttal and demanded that the evangelicals revoke their *Confession* and accept that they had been heard, refuted, and judged to be in error. Further he called for the criminal prosecution of, and possible military action against, any who refused to accept his demands. The emperor's complete rejection of the evangelical position was devastating and terrifying.

The evangelical princes responded by organizing themselves into a defensive alliance called the Schmalkaldic League and began looking for some new legal solution to their conundrum. What Kamm had asked hypothetically, they now faced in reality. If they failed to protect the proclamation of the true Gospel did they not risk God's great wrath? On the other hand, if they did oppose the emperor were they not in fact violating St. Paul's admonition in Romans 13 to be subject to temporal authority? Protestant leaders were also confronted with the unfortunate fact that in 1,500 years of church history resistance nearly always meant martyrdom. In fact, that is in principle exactly what Luther recommended to Kamm. Martyrdom, however, was not the solution that the princes were looking for.

Jurists from the Landgraviate of Hesse were the first to present a possible solution to Protestant princes' problem. These jurists claimed that the empire was not a monarchy but a constitutionally organized empire with electors and the emperor sharing power. Thus, when the protestant princes (some of whom were imperial electors) resisted enforcing his edict at Augsburg and who would resist with violence if

---

24 For a full discussion of the events that led up to the Augsburg *Confession* see Wilhelm Maurer, *Historical Commentary on the Augsburg Confession*, translated by H. George Anderson (Philadelphia: Fortress, 1986).

25 Mark D. Tranvik, trans., "The Confutation of the Augsburg Confession," in *Concord Sources*, 105–39.

necessary his attempts to implement that edict in their lands, they were not resisting a superior authority (such as Paul commanded one to obey) but instead they were resisting the actions of a sovereign of equal status.[26] The Hessian solution seemed convincing at first glance. In fact, Duke John of Saxony asked Martin Luther to comment on it.[27] Luther's appraisal of it was not nearly as positive as John's. Luther rejected the idea that the emperor and the electors were equals and told the princes that as Paul commanded, obedience was required.[28] The only option for the princes was martyrdom. This, again, was not what the princes were looking for. Desperate to find a solution, Duke John turned again to Gregor Brück.

Rather than attempting to argue that the emperor and the princes were equals, Brück argued that when a public official committed an act of "notorious injury" (such as a judge attempting to settle a legal matter in his own favor contrary to law, evidence, or precedent), then the official ceased to have jurisdiction in that matter. Brück's solution proved brilliant because it solved two problems in one stroke: it provided an answer to the problem of resisting the emperor while at the same time preventing general disorder and chaos. The emperor might be resisted in reference to his actions at the Diet of Augsburg and the attempt to regulate religion, but he remained sovereign in all other matters. He was, thus, the emperor in all things save that over which he never justly had jurisdiction—religion. For rulers concerned with justifying their own resistance but loathe to encourage rebellion in their own lands, Brück had delivered a workable legal and practical solution. John was encouraged. However, because of Luther's sharp rebuttal of the Hessian theory, he was unwilling to send Brück's opinion to Luther for comment. Instead, he summoned Luther to Torgau where Brück put the case to Luther in person.

---

26 Philip argued that the Golden Bull of 1356 supported his position that electors and the emperor jointly administered the empire. See *Politisches Archiv des Landgrafen Philipp des Grossmütigen von Hessen*, nr. 256: "This is the proscribed type German Nation we have in form and law, just as the Golden bull proclaims." While Philip does not state which portion of the Bull it is to which he is referring, he most likely has in mind section five. Section five concerns the rights of the Count Palatine and the Duke of Saxony to rule the empire in the interim following the death of one emperor and before the election of a new one.

27 *WABR* 5: 1510 and 1511, also *LW* 49: 254–5.

28 *LW* 49: 272–9.

Luther never accepted the ultimate conclusion of the Hessians that the electors and other magistrates were somehow equal to the emperor; he did, however, endorse the idea that the empire was not a monarchy but rather a constitutionally organized federation.[29] He was also largely, though with some reservations, convinced of Brück's argument regarding notorious injury. At the conclusion of the meeting in Torgau, what Luther and some of the other theologians there wrote has come to be called *The Torgau Declaration*. In it, they affirm that they have been convinced that within very tightly bound constitutional restrictions, civil and even military resistance could be allowable.[30] At the conclusion of the meeting, the Landgrave Philipp of Hesse asked Luther if he could expand upon what was in the *Torgau Declaration* for a more general audience. Luther answered the landgrave's request with the *Warning to His Dear German Nation* (Figure 7.1). The *Warning* depends on Luther's doctrine of the Two Kingdoms discussed above. As we have already seen, Luther argued that the two kingdoms had to be kept distinct; otherwise one would corrupt the other. This distinction became important during discussions of resistance because the emperor's attempts to regulate religion were understood by Luther and others as attempts by the secular realm to interfere in and meddle with the sacred realm.

Luther asserted three things in response to the emperor's attempts to meddle with the proclamation of the Gospel. First, he stated that the lawyers had convinced him of the constitutional right to resist. Second, he maintained that all subjects of the empire had a natural law right to self-defense. And third, he stated that the true proclamation of the Gospel was at risk in the current crisis. The natural law theory of resistance was based on the inborn instinct of all creatures

---

29 *WATR*: 3810, 4342, and 4380 (1538–1539), in all three *Table Talks*, Luther argues that the emperor was not a monarch, but that he ruled together with the electors.

30 *LW* 47: 8: "We are in receipt of a memorandum from which we learn that the doctors of law have come to an agreement on the question: In what situations may one resist the government? Since this possibility has now been established by these doctors and experts in the law, and since we certainly are in the kind of situation in which, as they show, resistance to the government is permissible, and since, further, we have always taught that one should acknowledge civil laws, submit to them, and respect their authority, inasmuch as the Gospel does not militate against civil laws, we cannot invalidate from Scripture the right of men to defend themselves even against the emperor in person, or anyone acting in his name."

Figure 7.1 Coverpage from Luther's *Warning to His Dear Germans*; Martin Luther, *Warnunge D. Martini Luther, An seine lieben Deudschen* (Straßburg, 1531). Reprinted by permission of the Bayerische Staatsbibliothek, Munich.

to defend themselves and their offspring against attack. The development of this line of thought stretches back to antiquity and provided much of the content for medieval just-war theory. In the *Warning to His Dear Germans*, Luther endorsed this line of thought:

> Furthermore, if war breaks out—which God forbid—I will not reprove those who defend themselves against the murderous and bloodthirsty papists, nor let anyone else rebuke them as being seditious.[31]

31 *LW* 47: 19.

Their actions are not seditious because these princes are, in fact, placing the emperor under the jurisdiction of the law. In a way, Luther is arguing that the law stands above even the emperor and upholding it honors true authority and is therefore not a violation of St. Paul's command to be subject to authority.[32] In the final section of the *Warning*, Luther made the case that the true proclamation of the Gospel was at risk by arguing that the emperor had become an agent of the pope and thus an abettor of the devil. A tyrant who attacked the proclamation of the Gospel and sided with Satan in Luther's words a "werewolf" who must be resisted.[33]

Luther thought that the situation in 1531 was markedly different from the one he spoke of to Kamm more than a decade earlier. However, his change of opinion regarding resistance versus martyrdom is rather significant and does raise an important question that must be addressed. Did Luther abandon some of his fundamental beliefs in order to accept resistance? Was he, in some ways, more dedicated to the political survival of his reforms than he was to his previous position? Was his position that 1531 was different from what he had told Kamm merely a function of the fact that he was now being confronted instead of Kamm with humiliation, punishment, and possible execution? Cynthia Shoenberger writes:

> To conclude then: having started from a position of complete opposition to resistance of any kind, Luther came eventually to embrace a notion of resistance . . . Certainly forcible resistance was meant to be a last resort and even then to be exercised in a carefully circumscribed manner; but it is significant that each time his church was in peril during the 1530s and 1540s, Luther did on one or another ground allow the possibility of resistance.[34]

This question is substantial and important because it goes to the heart of Luther's convictions about peace, justice, order, and obedience.

The question is not a new one, however. Luther was confronted with just this question. Soon after the publication of his *Warning*,

---

32 See Luther to Gregor Brück (5 August 1530), *LW* 49: 396.
33 *WA* 39: 41–2.
34 Cynthia Grant Shoenberger, "Luther and the Justifiability of Resistance to Legitimate Authority," *The Journal of the History of Ideas* 40 (1979): 19.

Luther received a letter from Lazarus Spengler (the chancellor of Nuremberg). Spengler was concerned that Luther had abandoned his position on obedience to the emperor. Luther writes back to Spengler and assures him of three things: first, his primary concern is ensuring that the Gospel can be preached, second, that he has not abandoned the fundamental position that authority ought to be obeyed, and third, that he has, though, been persuaded that the emperor has (through his own laws) allowed for resistance.

Thus, from his response to Spengler and from his other writings we may conclude a few important points regarding Luther's view of resistance to authority. First, Luther's primary concern was always that God must be served before man. This can be seen in how he viewed the work of the princes following the Diet of Augsburg and in his own life. The princes, he believed, took seriously the emperor's threat to stamp out reform. If they sat by and allowed this to happen they would be guilty of allowing the Gospel to be extinguished. They would have chosen to serve the emperor instead of God. From his own life, it is clear that while he argued that authority ought to be obeyed he always believed that this obedience is never blind. It has limits. In many letters to the Elector Frederick as well as in letters to Charles V and to the pope, Luther makes his position clear: he is willing to be obedient. However, he cannot and will not recant unless he can be shown his error by appealing to the scriptures.[35]

Second, Luther remains consistent in his position that the realms of God's creation (the secular and spiritual) must not be confused. For instance, Cargill Thompson states that when Luther deferred to the jurists on issues of the legality of resistance it was an abdication of his responsibility.[36] However, as a teacher of the Bible, it would

---

35 See, for example, Luther's letter to the Elector Frederick (3/7 or 8/1522) *LW* 48: 395–7: "I am returning not out of contempt for the authority of the Imperial Majesty or of Your Electoral Grace, or of any other government. Human authority is not always to be obeyed, namely, when it undertakes against the commandments of God . . . I know that this stay is without Your Electoral Grace's knowledge or consent. Your Electoral Grace is lord only of earthly goods and bodies, but Christ is the also the Lord of souls. To these he has sent me and for this [purpose] he has raised me up." For other examples, see Letters to Frederick (1/13–19/1519 *LW* 48: 103, 1/25/1521 *LW* 48: 195, 5/29/1523 *LW* 49: 35), to Charles V (4/28/1521 *LW* 48: 203), to the papal legate Cardinal Cajetan (10/18/1518, *LW* 48: 87), to Pope Leo X (1/5 or 6/1519, *LW* 48: 100).
36 Cargill Thompson, "Right of Resistance," 188.

have been inappropriate from Luther's perspective for him to declare that the jurists were wrong on such a fine point of jurisprudence.[37] The Two Kingdoms dialectic requires that people should act within their own area of competency. Luther's area of competency was the Bible, and not the laws of the empire. For him to declare that a jurist of such experience and skill as Brück would have been improper.

Luther sought across his career to sketch out a position between absolute obedience and complete disorder. Order and obedience are necessary and enable human communities to thrive. Sin and malfeasance are real and must be regulated by laws and sometimes the authority of the sword as administered by police and soldiers. Throughout all of his discussions, however, he maintains that God is the ultimate authority over all of life. When forced to decide between serving God or man, Luther argued that God must always be served. Often, for him, this meant being willing to accept martyrdom if it was laid before one. Sometimes, however, in very limited and circumscribed situations, one might also resist such tyranny with force. Thus, the caricatures of Luther with which we began this chapter as either a lackey of the princes or as a revolutionary are both grossly misleading.

---

37 One might ask why he was able to reject the Hessian theory so quickly and yet not judge the Saxon theory of notorious injury on the same merits. In reading his correspondence, it becomes clear that he believed the Hessian theory was simply so ridiculous that one needed neither legal training nor authority to determine that the emperor was a superior figure within the empire. One need not be a lawyer to determine that the President of the United States is a superior political authority to a city mayor or state governor, in other words.

CHAPTER 8

THE PEASANTS' WAR

The crisis of the Black Plague and its attendant population devasta-
tion brought to the surface resentments that had percolated below
the surface for generations. The peasant and serf were the lowest
of the three medieval classes of people and for hundreds of years
they had suffered in relative silence. When the plague decimated
their ranks, they began to demand better working conditions and
pay. The opposite happened. In England, for example, Parliament
passed legislation forbidding any increase in pay.[1] Similar legislation
was enacted in France. In Germany, there was no official legislation,
but there were increases in taxes. Beginning in 1381, peasants across
Europe began to revolt against their masters. The Englishman John
Ball gave the movement its slogan. He asked,

> When Adam delved
>   and Eve span,
> Who was then the Gentleman?

Ball was referring to Genesis and remarking that Adam had to toil
on the land and Eve spun clothes, so who exactly was the nobleman
(Figure 8.1)? Within in a few short years, the slogan had traveled to
Germany where it was translated, *Als Adam grab und Eva spann,
wo war denn da der Edelmann?* That phrase became so popular as a
slogan summarizing the resentment felt by even well-off people who
were not noble-born that the phrase was painted on the wall of the

---

1 1351 Statute of Labourers.

Figure 8.1 Adam Delved, MS K.26 St. John's College, Cambridge. Reprinted by permission of the Master and Fellows of St. John's College, Cambridge.

Augsburg weaver's hall in the fifteenth century.[2] For the less well-off, slogans eventually turned to violence.

THE CONDITION OF PEASANTS AROUND 1500
IN THE HOLY ROMAN EMPIRE

Where did peasant rage come from? In late medieval Germany, most peasants were *Hörige* or bondmen. They were free and so were not

---

2 Werner O. Packull, "In Search of the 'Common Man' in Early German Anabaptist Ideology," *Sixteenth Century Journal* 17/1 (1986).

slaves or serfs, but they did not own their land. Their land was subject to dues and fees paid to their lord. The fees and dues owed varied from place to place, but regardless of place these dues and taxes had increased across the fifteenth century. Dues and fees were also not based on yield. They were set. Should one suffer a crop loss due to weather or infestation, the fee was still owed. If one could not pay, the debt was assessed on later yields.[3] A second, lower, class of peasants were *Leibeigene*—serfs. These people owed all their service to their lord. They did work small tracts of land for their own crops, but could neither leave the land nor ever hope to more than subsistence. In most practical ways, there was little day-to-day difference between both groups. They scraped out a meager existence and owed much of the yield from their work to their manor's lord. Beyond normal taxes and dues, these peasant farmers owed special dues to the lord for seasonal events—a Christmas chicken, for example, and for major life events—a fee for each child born, another for baptism, one for marriage, and one for death. It was this death tax (*Todfall*) that was the most onerous. When any head of a household died, if he was a *Hörige*, his manorial lord was owed the dead man's most valuable piece of property. If the man was a serf, then the lord had the right to all of his possessions. In many places, the right to the best item (*Besthaupt*) was replaced by a monetary fee, but to pay that fee often amounted to the same thing because the peasant's family had to sell something to raise the money for the *Todfall*. When the Swabian peasants wrote a summary of their complaints in 1525, they demanded that the "*Todfall* be abolished."

Whether one was a completely free land-owning peasant, a bondman, or a serf, he also owed dues and fees to the church. The church fees were called tithes. The concept of a tithe (a tenth) comes from the Old Testament and was a gift to God in thanksgiving for all that one had received from God's bounty over the year. By the medieval era, the tithe had actually evolved into three dues owed to the church. The great tithe was a fee of 10 percent of the grain harvest and wine production. The "lesser tithe" was a fee of 10 percent on fruit and

---

3 One of the demands of the Memmingen peasants in 1525 was a reduction in annual fees if a hail or other destructive force from "God, the almighty," destroyed their crops. See, Franz Ludwig Baumann, ed., *Akten Zur Geschichte Des Deutschen Bauernkrieges Aus Oberschwaben* (Freiburg: Herder'sche Verlagshandlung, 1877), 125.

vegetables. The final tithe was a "blood tithe" on animals. Between the taxes, fees, and dues owed to one's manorial lord and the three tithes owed to the church, a peasant was forced to survive on perhaps less than 40 percent of what he actually grew. At the same time, the lords and church officials above him looked on him with absolute and near total contempt. A joke about the peasants said that they are "Just like an ox, but without the horns."[4]

While those above them looked upon them with scorn, their reciprocal duties were actually waning. At one point, the exchange between peasant and lord actually did have mutual benefits and duties. A peasant toiled and the lord protected. By the 1520s, imperial law and jurisdiction within the Holy Roman Empire had largely eliminated the need for peasants to be protected from roaming and ravaging hoards. Thus, the lord expected more and more from the peasant, looked down upon him with contempt, but offered him little or nothing in exchange for his work. This was a recipe for not only anger and resentment, but violence.

THE PEASANTS' WAR OF 1525

The Peasants' War of 1525 was not the first outbreak of peasant violence. As we noted at the very beginning of this chapter, peasants in England erupted in the 1380s. In the Holy Roman Empire there were a series of uprisings. Perhaps the most famous precursor to 1525 was the revolt led by the "Drummer of Niklashausen." In 1476, the uneducated peasant shepherd and drummer, Hans Behem, declared that he had a vision from the Virgin Mary. Mary declared to him that there were to be no authorities here on earth among people, because all are equal before God. Taxes, the Virgin added, were unjust and were to be abolished. Private property was likewise unjust and therefore all property ought to be held in common. By all accounts, Behem was an enthusiastic and persuasive preacher. At the height of his movement he had upwards of 35,000 peasants marching in his cause. He called for the execution of all clergy and any secular lords who refused to dissolve their property and join the common men. The bishop of Würzberg, who was Niklashausen's secular and

---

4 Herwig Ebner, "Der Bauer in Der Mittelalterlichen Historiographie," in *Bäuerliche Sachkultur Des Spätmittelalters* (Vienna: Österreichische Akademie der Wissenschaften, 1984), 95.

ecclesiastical lord, reacted with ferocity. The peasants were attacked. Their march shattered and Behem was burned at the stake on 19 July 1476. In 1493, peasants in Alsace rebelled under the banner of the *Bundschuh*. The *Bundschuh* (Figure 8.2) was the peasant's shoe. It was a simple leather slipper that tied up the front. It became an emblem of their fight and their plight. Images of the peasant shoe were sown onto banners carried by rebelling peasants. The Alsatian peasants were also crushed, but the *Bundschuh* symbol survived. A 1502 *Bundschuh* rebellion near Speyer sought to overthrow both secular and ecclesiastical lords. When the movement had been defeated its leaders stated, after being tortured, that one of their main objectives

Figure 8.2 A peasant holding a "freedom" banner from Thomas Murner's *Von dem grossen Lutherischen Narren*; Thomas Murner, *Uon dem grossen Lutherischen Narren wie in doctor Murner beschworen hat. [et]c.* (Straßburg, 1522). Reprinted by permission of the Bayerische Staatsbibliothek, Munich.

was to "never again pay a tithe, either to the clergy or to the lords and nobility."[5]

The earliest outbreak of the 1525 Peasants' War actually began in the Fall of 1524. According to the legends surrounding the events, a count's wife demanded during the harvest season that her peasants and serfs collect fruit and snails for her. Leaving their harvest in the fields at such a time was dangerous because any sudden storm could wreck an entire seasons work. The peasants reacted almost viscerally to the request. Quickly, the peasants directly affected rallied many others to their cause. By mid-September they had even organized enough so that they had identified a former imperial soldier as their leader; Hans Müller. By October, the movement had made its first real religious move when peasants led by Müller and others came to the aid of peasants in Waldshut. The pastor of Waldshut was Balthasar Hubmaier. Hubmaier was an initial follower of Zwingli and had read Luther. The bishop overseeing Waldshut attempted to remove him from the parish, but he was popular with the common people and they rose to his defense. As they rose to defend him, he also defended their claims against unjust economic policies and linked the peasant cause to religious reform.

Over the winter, peasant discontent did not die away as it had in other years. Instead it accelerated. The turning point for the event of the Peasants' War seems to be Carnival season leading up to Lent. It is a riotous season that by tradition calls into question, often in a mocking way, social and political norms. In 1525, the jovial nature of Carnival hit a different nerve: anger and grievance.

The grievances of the peasants during this time were best summarized by a collection of peasants in Swabia, in southern Germany near the Swiss cantons. Traditionally, their treatise has been called the "Twelve Articles of the Peasants." The treatise was issued by the "Christian Union of Upper Swabia" in March 1525 with the title, "The basic and just articles of the whole peasantry, concerning the difficulties with ecclesiastical and secular authorities by whom they feel themselves burdened."[6] The pamphlet had 11 articles and a

---

5 Gerald Strauss, *Manifestations of Discontent in Germany on the Eve of the Reformation* (Bloomington,: Indiana University Press, 1971), 146.

6 See *The Twelve Articles of Upper Swabia*, in Günther Franz (ed.), *Quellen zur Geschichte des Bauernkrieges* (Darmstadt: Oldenbourg, 1963), 174–9. Reprinted in Scott and Scribner, *German Peasants' War*, 252–7.

conclusion. The articles present the peasants' grievances in a way that was easily understood and thus quickly became popular. More than 25,000 copies were printed in the spring of 1525. The *Articles* are a response to critics who blamed the peasants for revolting and for misusing the Gospel to aid their rebellion. They state that both accusations are false. First, they claim that they are not rebelling. All that they seek is a formal redress of their just grievances. Second, they claim that they are simple Christians who are seeking to follow the Gospel and use the Bible as the measure of their requests. Not completely naïve about their situation, they end the introduction to the *Articles* with a veiled threat reminding their lords that God heard the cries of the Israelites in Egypt and God will hear their cries as well.

In using the Bible as standard and norm for the life of the community, the peasants hoped to connect their program with the Wittenberg and Zurich reformations. The text itself is full of marginal references to applicable scripture prooftexts. The *Twelve Articles* are really 12 demands. The demands encompass the nature of the Peasants' War as an economic-political-religious event. The line between religious demands and political or economic demands is blurred almost completely in the *Twelve Articles*.

First, they demand a right to call their own pastors. Instead of assignment by a bishop, the community ought to be able to hire and fire their pastor. The standard by which the pastor would be evaluated was his correspondence to the "pure and clear" Gospel. Thus the first demand is entirely religious and reflects the events in Waldshut and other places. The second demand was both religious and economic. They acknowledge the just nature of God's requirement for a tithe, but believe that tithes have been unjustly and unbiblically administered. Thus, they seek the abolishment of the lesser tithes (on fruits and animals) and a local administration of the greater tithe on grain. The third demand harkens back to John Ball's rallying cry by noting that Christ died for all men and therefore all men should be free. Serfdom and bound labor, whether through dues or fees, should be eliminated. Next they call for the freedom to gather wood in the forests, fish from the streams, and the restitution of communal land. Each of these demands are supported by biblical warrant. For example, the freedom to fish is supported by the Genesis account wherein God gives all men, not just some, dominion over creation. They also demand a reduction in the obligations owed to feudal lords and that peasants be paid for their work on behalf of their lords and their lords honor their agreements. The eighth demand focused on unjust increases in dues, fees and rents. Here the peasants are not only reacting against unjust taxes but the entire system that demanded from them equal rents and fees on their yield regardless of whether it was a good year or not. In the ninth, they complain that new laws governing their behavior have been administered capriciously and that in the future criminal punishments should fit the crime committed. Returning in ten and eleven to purely economic issues, they demand that community property be administered by the community and not by the lord who has used this authority to unjustly forbid peasants from utilizing this common land and finally the abolishment of the *Todfall*. The last article is not a demand but a declaration that if one or more of their articles were contrary to scripture they would revoke it. This statement was clearly crafted, in that they wish to be judged in all that they said and did by the Bible, to conjure up the (even by 1525) iconic image of Luther's stand against the emperor at Worms.

By late spring 1525, the movement spread to encompass most of Franconia and Thuringia in southern Germany and was beginning to spread into west and north toward Hesse and Saxony. It was in Thuringia that the expanding peasant revolt met up with the itinerant preacher and scholar Thomas Müntzer. In the spring of 1525, Thomas Müntzer was the pastor of Mühlhausen. But, he was more than just the city's pastor. Through the creation of a new town governing body called the "Eternal Council" that was ordered on Müntzer's understanding of Divine Law he exerted control over the affairs of the city as well. To compliment the work of the Eternal Council, Müntzer organized the "Eternal League of God." This was to be the city's military force. Müntzer was convinced that God had called him to purify the church and the land of unrighteousness and the Eternal Council and the Eternal League would help him in this mission. When Luther learned about what Müntzer was doing in Mühlhausen he felt that Müntzer was attempting to establish a theocracy in Mühlhausen and was preparing to spread that rule elsewhere. In a letter to Nicholas von Amsdorf in Magdeburg, Luther refers to Müntzer as the "king and emperor of Mühlhausen."[7]

---

7 *WABR* 3: 472.

When the Peasants' War reached Mühlhausen, Thomas Müntzer was prepared to aid it and encourage it because he felt that the peasants were his allies in extinguishing injustice and enforcing righteousness. By that time his Eternal League had roughly 600 men and a new standard to rally around—a flag with a rainbow (a symbol of God's protection) and the phrase "The Word of God endures Forever." The Eternal League's first campaign was a great letdown. The League marched to the nearby city of Langensalza, but when they got there they discovered that the city council and the local peasants had already reached an accord. Disappointedly, the League marched back to Mühlhausen. Along the way they sacked monasteries, a few churches, and some other property. As we shall see below, it was the sacking of monasteries, convents, churches, and other lands that led Luther to write his most vigorous essays on the Peasants War.

Müntzer, meanwhile, continued his campaign. On 29 April, Müntzer promised the City of Frankenhausen (which had written requesting 200 men for support) that "everyone, everyone, as many as we have, wants to come to you, marching through all the country-side and on the way placing ourselves at your disposal."[8] In May 1525, Müntzer set out from Mühlhausen to engage Count Ernst of Mansfeld who was attempting to regain control of Frankenhausen. Despite Müntzer's enthusiastic claims that everyone was willing to help, the vast majority of the Mühlhausen peasants did not join him in his march. Reports that the Landgrave Phillip of Hesse was bringing an army to aid Ernst of Mansfeld had already made it to Mühlhausen and many peasants seemed to have recognized, even if he could not, that Thomas Müntzer was leading his army toward disaster.

Müntzer was able to make it to Frankenhausen without incident and entered the city in a triumphant march. From outside the city, Albrecht of Mansfeld (another prince) sought a peaceful solution to increasingly dangerous situation. Compromise was not what Müntzer was after, however. He sought the unconditional surrender of the princes and promised them that he would destroy them all if they did not heed his calls. As if to reinforce his message, he had Albrecht's messengers executed as spies. Following the execution, Müntzer began a series of sermons on the just nature of the peasants' cause and the righteous anger God would pour out upon the princes. Following the

---

8 Thomas Müntzer, *The Collected Works of Thomas Muntzer*, trans. Peter Matheson (Edinburgh: T & T Clark, 1988), 144.

sermons, the peasants began to sing together the hymn "Come, Holy Spirit." While the peasants sang, the princes attacked. The Battle of Frankenhausen was over before it started. By the end of the day nearly 6,000 peasants were killed, while 6 of the princes' soldiers were wounded. The peasants were surrounded on all sides. Count Phillip von Solms recorded the events of the day in a letter to his son:

> We brought our guns up the slope so that they could fire into [the peasants], and attacked the nearest of them with horse and foot. They did not hold firm, but ran to seek the safety of the town. We gave pursuit and killed the majority of them between the hill and the town, but many got inside. We began to storm the town at once and conquered it speedily, and killed everyone caught there.[9]

Müntzer survived the day, though. He must have been one of the men who made it into the city during the rout, because he was found in bed feigning ignorance of the day's events and claiming to be ill. He was arrested, tortured, confessed, recanted, and then turned over to Ernst of Mansfeld. On 27 May 1525, Müntzer was beheaded at Mühlhausen for treason. His head was placed on a pike as a warning to others.

In all, the Peasants' War was a disaster for peasants. Counts, nobles, and other lords did not stop at the walls of Frankenhausen. They sought to put down the rebellion such that it might never rise again. Villages were laid waste. Fields were burned. Peasants were slaughtered. Contemporary estimates put the total killed in the war at 100,000. Once the war was over taxes and rents on the peasants were increased so that the lords could pay off the debts they accumulated during the campaign. Georg Spalatin wrote at the time that "of hangings and beheadings there is no end."[10] Many then and even many today lay considerable blame for the violence during and after the Peasants' War on Martin Luther.

MARTIN LUTHER AND THE PEASANTS' WAR

Martin Luther published, over a three-month period, five responses to the Peasants' War. Understanding each writing and its context will

---

9 "Count Phillip von Solms's report to his son Reinhard, 16 May 1525." In Scott, *Peasants' War*, 290–1.

10 Köstlin and Kawerau, *Martin Luther: Sein Leben Und Seine Schriften*, 714.

allow us to understand and appreciate Luther's perspective on the war. He was neither the monster he was declared then nor is he a hapless victim of circumstance. His perspective on the war changed and evolved as, frankly, the situation in the war changed and evolved.

Luther's first foray into discussing the Peasants' War was in mid-April. At this point he had heard little or nothing about the more violent aspects of the war. As we noted earlier the beginning months of the war had more in common with a general strike than an outright war. He was asked in early April to comment upon the *Twelve Articles* written by the Swabian peasants. They sought his opinion and he gave it. It is measured in tone and largely supportive of the peasants in character. On the title page he put a quotation from Psalm 7 aimed directly at the nobility, "His mischief shall return upon his own head, and his violent dealing shall come down upon his own pate" (7.16, KJV). Clearly, Luther believed that the nobility were responsible for the current sad state of affairs. Had they dealt with their people more justly none of this would have happened. Luther titled the treatise *Ermahnung zum Frieden auf die zwölf Artikel der Bauernschaft in Swaben.*[11] It is often translated, *Admonition to Peace a Reply to the Twelve Articles of the Peasants in Swabia.*[12] What can be a bit lost in this translation is the rebuking and warning nature of the admonition. This is not a gentle reproof. This is a scolding and a warning.

Luther begins by addressing the nobility. He puts the blame for the current situation clearly at their feet, "We have no one on earth to blame for this disastrous rebellion, except you princes and lords, and especially you blind bishops and mad priests and monks, whose hearts are hardened, even to this present day."[13] Luther believed that the peasants actions were the result of noble greed and God's punishment for such greed. Luther does not doubt that the lords have the power to suppress the peasants, but he warns them against such action and instead encourages them to "become different men."[14] To the first proposal of the peasants, he tells the lords that they have no business preventing the common people from hearing the word of God from a pastor of their choosing. The other articles, he says, are

---

11 *WA* 18: 291–334.
12 *LW* 46: 17–43.
13 *LW* 46: 18.
14 *LW* 46: 20.

economic in nature and that the peasants are right to protest against economic abuse. Luther writes,

> The other articles protest economic injustices, such as the death tax. These protests are also right and just, for rulers are not appointed to exploit their subjects for their own profit and advantage, but to be concerned about the welfare of their subjects. And the people cannot tolerate it very long if their rulers set confiscatory tax rates and tax them out of their very skins. What good would it do a peasant if his field bore as many gulden as stalks of wheat if the rulers only taxed him all the more and then wasted it as though it were chaff to increase their luxury, and squandered his money on their own clothes, food, drink, and buildings? Would not the luxury and the extravagant spending have to be checked so that a poor man could keep something for himself?[15]

Luther concludes his warning and exhortation to the princes by noting that the peasants have published not only the *Twelve Articles* but other grievances as well. Luther believes that the princes should pay attention to these complaints and seek to ameliorate them. He then turns to speak to the peasants. He also rebukes and warns them.

Luther begins this section by telling the peasants that he does see the just nature of their cause but then quickly turns to warn them to be careful, "Nevertheless, you, too, must be careful that you take up your cause justly and with a good conscience."[16] They must be careful because there are rebellious preachers at large in the world that would try and provoke the peasants to violence. He states that they must not resort to violence. First, because God has commanded that all men be subject to authority by citing Romans 13. But also more importantly because they have claimed for themselves the title of a "Christian brotherhood." As a "Christian brotherhood," they cannot resort to violence.[17] Even if their rulers are unjust, that "does

---

15 *LW* 46: 22.

16 *LW* 46: 23.

17 Many students who encounter Luther on the Peasants' War for the first time view his actions as deeply hypocritical. They ask why it is permissible for him to resist the emperor and it is not permissible for the peasants to do the same. As we shall see below, the fundamental difference Luther saw between his resistance and the peasants' was violence. Luther believed, though this could have been debated then, that he was still

not excuse disorder and rebellion, for the punishing of wickedness is not the responsibility of everyone, but of the worldly rulers who bear the sword."[18] If they do resort to violence, or worse, killing then they have in fact committed a more egregious sin. It is one thing, Luther says, to take from a man the harvest of his sweat and toil. It is another thing entirely to take his life. Murder and pillage are also forbidden not only by God but by the simple and straightforward laws of nature and the empire. For Luther, breaking the law, destroying property, and killing men are not the way to solve human problems. He finishes on a practical note. If the peasants resort to violence, they will be met by greater force and violence. This will destroy rather than advance their cause. Thus for theological, legal, and practical reasons, Luther exhorts the peasants to find a peaceful resolution to their grievances.

He then turns to examine the individual articles. The first article he finds just and reiterates what he said to the princes—that the peasants ought to be able to find and choose a godly pastor. He completely rejects the peasants second article on the tithe. The tithe is a requirement going back to the Old Testament. He views any attempt to overturn it as a not-too-subtle attempt to steal what is not theirs. In the third article on the abolition of bondage, he is equally harsh. The peasants claim that villeinage is now forbidden because Christ has set all men free. For Luther, this is wrong both exegetically and theologically. When Luther reads the Bible, he notes that even great Patriarchs like Abraham owned slaves. Thus, slavery cannot be forbidden. But, even if this were not the case, the peasants have misunderstood the theology of Christian freedom from Luther's perspective. A Christian can be completely free in Christ and yet remain even in chains in a prison. The freedom Christ offers is not freedom from physical bondage but from the bondage to sin and devil. Christ offers the freedom of salvation which is spiritual. For Luther, this was a far greater freedom than any physical freedom. Many have criticized Luther for this perspective, but he was really little different than most men of his age. Philip Melanchthon, Martin Bucer, and

---

involved in a legal dispute and that the Edict of Worms had been stayed a number of times. Therefore, he was not actively rebelling against the emperor. More importantly, however, he did not resort to violence and had rejected offers (from Ulrich von Hutten for example) from knights who had pledged to defend him to the death.

18 *LW* 46: 26.

others all wrote similarly harsh words on the idea that Christian freedom meant that all men were equal. On the economic articles, Luther had previously noted their justice and here says that he will not speak more on the topic because he is not an expert on these matters and leaves them up to those who have competence in that area. He ends by noting that both sides would have to compromise in order to maintain peace. To the princes he states, "stop being so stubborn! You will finally have to stop being such oppressive tyrants—whether you want to or not. Give these poor people room in which to live and air to breath."[19] He then immediately turns to the peasants and tells them to "give up the excessive demands of some of your articles."[20] If both sides give a little, then peace will be maintained and a more just society will surely result. If they do not, then he fears things will turn terribly violent.

A few days after he wrote the *Admonition*, he received a copy of the Wiengarten Treaty. This treaty was an agreement between the Swabian League and the peasants of Upper (meaning southern, near the Alps, and therefore farther up the Rhine River) Swabia. By mid-April the peasants had an army of nearly 12,000 men, some of whom had been mercenaries in the past and so knew how to fight in a battle. The League's army was led by George Truchsess von Waldburg and he had about 7,000 men. Waldburg recognized the difficulty and loss of life that would be involved in any battle and so negotiated rather generous terms with the peasants. They agreed to return home and cease their violence. He agreed to establish a commission that would oversee a just and fair hearing and arbitration of their grievances. Luther saw the willingness of each side to give and to enter into negotiations as a positive development. He quickly penned a preface and a postscript to the Weingarten Treaty and saw that it was published with the text of the treaty rather quickly.

However, as we saw earlier in this chapter, just as things seemed to glimmer hope, the Peasants' War erupted more violently and energetically in Franconia and Thuringia. Luther witnessed some of these more violent uprisings and once during a sermon he was shouted down. The record is unclear whether or not he was assaulted at all in the fracas that ensued, but we do know that he was very much shaken by the experience. News reports also began reaching

19 *LW* 46: 43.
20 *LW* 46: 43.

the north of Germany that reported the destruction of castles, monasteries, and abbeys. As Luther returned home to Wittenberg, his views of the peasants shifted. The justness of the cause does not excuse violence. Ever. Luther feared, justly it might be argued, that chaos, riot, and pillage always hurt the weak much more than the powerful, the innocent more than the guilty. From his perspective, God would not countenance the raping and pillaging that was taking place within the empire. God had established the sword to condemn the wicked. On 6 May, the morning after he returned to Wittenberg he put to pen his thoughts on the peasants rioting. He called the short work, "Against the Storming Peasants [*Wider die Stürmenden bawren*]." It was a blistering attack,

> they are starting a rebellion, and are violently robbing and plundering monasteries and castles which are not theirs . . . [R]ebellion is not just simple murder it is like a great fire which attacks and devastates the whole land. Thus rebellion brings with it a land filled with murder and bloodshed it makes widows and orphans, and turns everything upside down, like the worst disaster. Therefore let anyone who can, smite, slay, stab, secretly or openly remembering that nothing is more poisonous, hurtful, or Devilish than a rebel. It is just as when one must kill a mad dog; if you do not strike him, he will strike you, and the whole land with you.[21]

The text was given to Joseph Klug, one of Wittenberg's printers. Luther intended, I would argue, to distinguish between the violent peasants that needed to be stopped and the just causes of the peasants that did not resort to rioting and murder. In fact, he had Klug publish the short tract as an addendum to the longer treatise on the *Twelve Articles*. The title page of the new combined work bears this out. It continues the same title page as the earlier edition that contained just his response to the *Twelve Articles* but adds a new subtitle.[22] The new title page now reads, *Admonition to Peace a Reply to the Twelve Articles of the Peasants in Swabia. Also, against the Robbing and Murdering Hoards of the Other Peasants* (Figure 8.3).

---

21 *LW* 46: 50.
22 Flug simply put the new title in smaller lettering and added the new subtitle. Aside from that, he also translated the Psalm text from Latin into German. No other changes to the title page were made.

Figure 8.3 Coverpage from the first edition of *Against the Robbing and Murdering Hoards of the Other Peasants*; Martin Luther, *Ermanunge zum fried auff die zwelff artickel der Bawrschafft ynn Schwaben. Auch widder die reubischen und mördisschen rotten der andern bawren* (Wittenberg, 1525). Reprinted by permission of the Universitäts- und Landesbibliothek Sachsen-Anhalt.

The implication is plain; the murdering, robbing, rioting peasants are different from the peasants discussed in the *Admonition*. This distinction, however, was almost immediately lost. When the text was published in Erfurt a week or so later, it was published without the *Admonition* but still carried the all-important "other." By the time it

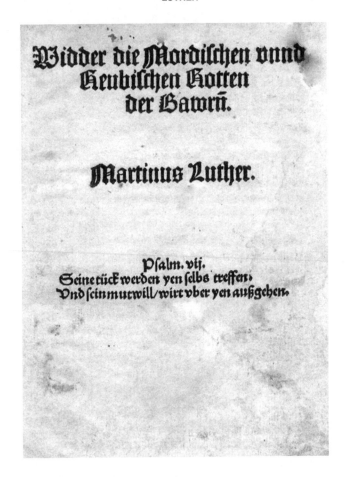

Figure 8.4 Coverpage from the Mainz edition of *Against the Murdering and Robbing Hoards of the Peasants*; Martin Luther, *Widder die Mordischen unnd Reubischen Rotten der Bawrn* (Mainz, 1525). Reprinted by permission of the Universitäts- und Landesbibliothek Sachsen-Anhalt.

was published in Leipzig, Mainz, Nuremberg, and other cities the "other" also disappeared (Figure 8.4). All of those editions came out after the fateful Battle of Frankenhausen. It now appeared to many that Luther wrote the treatise to justify what had happened in Frankenhausen. The line "smit, slay, stab," makes this assumption easy. For example, Hermann Mühlpfort who was a supporter of Luther's, wrote to a friend in Wittenberg:

> In my opinion there was no pressing need for this hasty tract. There was enough murdering of peasants, burghers, women, and children taking place; not only were the poor folk being killed, but also their goods and possessions were being taken from their innocent wives and children and burnt. God knows, these same knights are supposed to be the children of God! But we should have more pity for the poor, need, and simple folk who were misled by Thomas and others.[23]

Because people believed that Luther wrote the treatise after Frankenhausen, few believed that Luther was actually horrified by the reports of what happened there. Initially, Luther ignored those who said that he supported what happened at Frankenhausen. Perhaps he thought that idea too ludicrous an accusation to merit a response. Instead, he focused his energy on the one person he believed was actually responsible for Frankenhausen: Thomas Müntzer.

On 15 May 1525, as the peasant army he led was being slaughtered by the thousands, Thomas Müntzer snuck away from his followers and hid himself within the city. He was found later in the day hiding in a bed in a house near the city gate. At first he denied being Müntzer, but when a satchel of letters was found in the room, he confessed. Luther learned of the events in Frankenhausen and probably got copies of Müntzer's letters from his friend Johan Rühl who was an aid to Count Albrecht. Rühl also enclosed a letter by Müntzer in which he placed the blame for the events of May squarely on the shoulders of the peasants and accepted no responsibility for what happened himself. Luther published Müntzer's letters together with marginal notes so that he could unmask what he saw as Müntzer's treachery.

Any hope that publishing Müntzer's letters would help contextualize his writing on the murdering and robbing peasants was unrealized, however. In fact, many people believed that the publication of Müntzer's letters predated the tract on the murdering hoards. In that context, the publication of the letters seems to set up the fiery and blistering *Murdering Hoards*. Frustrated by the continuing confusion

---

23 Tom Scott and Bob Scribner, eds., *The German Peasants' War: A History in Documents* (Atlantic Heights, NJ: Humanities Press, 1991), 322.

about his true opinion and his actions regarding the peasants, Luther preached a sermon on the subject in Wittenberg in early June. That did not quiet any of the controversy however. Finally, in mid-July, he published a justification of his actions.[24] It is a justification and is not, in any fashion, an apology or a retraction.

Luther is, in fact, unapologetic saying at one point that all that matters is whether or not what he said was in accord with the witness of scripture, "If it pleases God, I do not really care whether you like it or not."[25] How could such slaughter please God, one might justly ask. At this point, Luther argues that the peasants sought mercy when they gave none themselves. Further, they do not deserve mercy any more than a common murderer deserves mercy. Worse, from his perspective, they say they deserve mercy because Christ was merciful. Luther now presents one of the most important clarifications of his thought on secular authority that he will ever offer. For Luther, Christian mercy *cannot* and *should not* extend to the judicial realm of society. Christian mercy is a spiritual gift from God when he forgives sinful people. It can even be an act of piety between people. What it cannot be is a judicial or legal possibility. Why? Because, this would let injustice, deceit, murder, and mayhem prosper and flourish:

Suppose I were to break into a man's house, rape his wife and daughters, break open his strong box, take his money, put a sword to his chest, and say, "If you will not put up with this, I shall run you through, for you are a godless wretch"; then if a crowd gathered and were about to kill me, or if the judge ordered my head off, suppose I were to cry out, "Hey, Christ teaches you to be merciful and not to kill me," what would people say?

That is exactly what these peasants and their sympathizers are now doing. Now that they have, like robbers, murderers, thieves, and scoundrels, done what they pleased to their masters, they want to put on a song and dance about mercy, and say, "Be merciful, as Christ teaches, and let us rage, as the devil teaches: do good to us, and let us do our worst to you; be satisfied with what we have done and call it right, and call what you are doing wrong." Who would not like to get away with that? If that is mercy, then we shall institute a pretty state of affairs; we shall have no

---

24 *LW* 46: 57–86.
25 *LW* 46: 66.

sword, ruler, punishment, hangman, or prison, and let every scoundrel do as he pleases; then, when he is to be punished, we shall sing, "Hey, be merciful, as Christ teaches." That would be a fine way of doing things![26]

Thus, for Luther, the cry for mercy is actually not a cry for mercy but a cry that seeks to overturn justice. In such a world the weak would always suffer at the hands of the strong. This, of course, does not excuse the violent reactions of the nobility. Luther states that once the peasants surrendered they should have been dealt with far less harshly than to be savagely cut down. Running down surrendering peasants was no less murder than when peasants struck down surrendering lords. His anger is clear as he recounts an exchange between a knight and Müntzer's pregnant widow:

[He] fell on one knee before her, and said, "Dear lady, let me * * * you." O a knightly, noble deed, done to a poor, helpless, pregnant little woman! That is a brave hero for you! He is worth three knights, at the very least! Why should I write for scoundrels and hogs like that? The Scriptures call such people "beasts" [Tit. 1.12], that is, "wild animals," such as wolves, boars, bears, and lions, and I shall not make men of them; and yet we must put up with them, when God plagues us with them. I had two fears. If the peasants became lords, the devil would become abbot; but if these tyrants became lords, the devil's mother would become abbess. Therefore I wanted to do two things: quiet the peasants, and instruct the pious lords. The peasants were unwilling to listen, and now they have their reward; the lords, too, will not hear, and they shall have their reward also. However, it would have been a shame if they had been killed by the peasants; that would have been too easy a punishment for them. Hell-fire, trembling, and gnashing of teeth [Matt. 22.13] in hell will be their reward eternally, unless they repent.[27]

CONCLUSION

Luther's reaction to the Peasants' War undoubtedly hurt the progress of his wing of the Reformation among the peasants. Many of them

---

26 *LW* 46: 68.
27 *LW* 46: 84.

believed that he had abandoned them to the savagery of the nobility. He took years to recognize that fact. What he did not do was change his perspective on violence and disorder. He saw both as the handiwork of the devil. In many ways, the results of the Peasants' War seem to bear this out. There were no real appreciable gains for the peasants and though there were a number of lords and nobles who were killed in the initial stages of the revolt, once the nobles had time to organize the peasant armies had little chance of success. By the end of the year, more than 100,000 men, women, and children had been killed. Thousands of others were orphaned and widowed. What Luther saw when he looked around was a situation that was markedly worse for many peasants. His initial hopes for mediated arbitration came to nothing. The violence of late April and early May overwhelmed any chance for that type of solution.

CHAPTER 9

LUTHER: ON THE JEWS

In 1535, Martin Luther began to lecture on the book of Genesis. He would take the next ten years to complete the lecture series. It is his last major endeavor as the professor of Old Testament at the University of Wittenberg. In November 1536, he turned his attention to Genesis 9. In Genesis 9, the great flood waters that covered the earth recede and Noah and his family leave their ark. After they receive the blessing of God and a promise from God to never again destroy the earth, Noah plants a vineyard, creates a drink from the fruit of the vine and gets drunk. He falls asleep naked and is discovered by his son Ham. For centuries, theologians and bible professors sought to excuse Noah's drunken stupor. The most common explanation for why Noah got drunk was that he did not know the alcoholic power of the fermented grape and so one must forgive Noah's mistaken drunkenness. When Luther turned to lecture on this interesting story, he had no time for such explanations. According to Luther, Noah did know the power of the vine and his drunkenness was sinful. This sinfulness reminds Christians, "who know their weakness and for this reason are disheartened, to take comfort in the offense that comes from the account of the lapses among the holiest and most perfect patriarchs. In such instances we should find sure proof of our own weakness and therefore bow down in humble confession, not only to ask for forgiveness but also to hope for it."[1] Over the centuries, many interpreters of Luther have similarly tried various explanations to account for Luther's offensive and shameful treatise, *On the Jews and Their Lies*. In this chapter we will examine Luther's early treatise on Jews, the 1523 treatise *That Jesus Christ was Born a Jew*,

---

1 Luther, *Lectures on Genesis* (1544), *LW* 2: 166; *WA* 42: 378.

the 1543 treatise *On the Jews and Their Lies*, and end by examining the explanations that have been most often forwarded as reasons for Luther's tone and tenor in *Lies*.

LUTHER AND THE JEWS IN THE 1520s:
THAT JESUS CHRIST WAS BORN A JEW

In order to understand Luther's 1523 treatise, *That Jesus Christ was Born a Jew*, we must actually begin more than 15 years earlier with a controversy that erupted over the use of books written in Hebrew by Jewish rabbis and their use by Christian scholars and teachers. Sometime before 1507, a Jewish butcher in Cologne converted to Christianity and came into close contact with the local Dominican monastery. Over the next few years, Johannes Pfefferkorn published, with the help of his Dominican allies, a number of tracts against Jewish literature where he repudiated some of the more ghastly rumors spread about Jews in the late medieval era but also called for the confiscation and burning of Hebrew literature as anti-Christian and heretical.[2] By 1509, Pfefferkorn, again through the Cologne Dominicans, secured from the Holy Roman Emperor Maximilian, an order for such a collection. A small controversy erupted and Maximilian appointed the archbishop of Mainz to present to him a learned opinion on the subject. Uriel von Gemmingen, the archbishop, sought input from a number of places but most significantly from Jacob von Hockstraten, the papal inquisitor in Cologne and the prior of the Dominican monastery there (Pfefferkorn was actually his assistant), and Johannes Reuchlin a judge and law professor from Tübingen. As well as being known for his legal knowledge, Reuchlin was also a famous philologist and the author of an early Hebrew grammar book. In 1511, Reuchlin published his opinion on the matter in a book titled *Augenspiegel* (Eyeglasses).[3] In 1513, Hockstraten formally charged Reuchlin with heresy and ordered his works be confiscated.

The so-called Pfefferkorn Controversy is important to our understanding of Luther and his views regarding Jews because it is one of the earliest events in which we learn of Luther's views toward Jews

---

2 Johannes Pfefferkorn, *Der Juden Spiegel* (Nuremberg: 1507).

3 Johannes Reuchlin, *Doctor Johannsen Reuchlins . . . Augenspiegel* (Tubingen: Thomas Anshelm, 1511). It has recently been published in English, Johannes Reuchlin, *Recommendation Whether to Confiscate, Destroy, and Burn All Jewish Book*, trans. Peter Wortsman (Mahwah, NJ: Paulist Press, 2000).

and Jewish literature. The Pfefferkorn Controversy divided many theological faculties and led Ulrich von Hutten to publish a farcical work, *Letters of Obscure Men*, in which he mocked those who attacked Reuchlin. In a 1514 letter to one of his closest friends, George Spalatin, Luther makes clear that he supported Reuchlin's position. Luther writes,

> Ortwin [another antagonist of Reuchlin] heedlessly distorts the words and meanings of the definitely innocent Reuchlin, but because through all this raving he increases the damage of blindness and obstinacy in his heart, as Scripture says, "He burdens himself with heavy mud." In corresponding with you, I could laugh at many details if it were not that one should rather weep over than laugh at such great depravity of souls. I am afraid we shall have more of this. May God quickly end it. One thing, however, pleases me: namely, that this matter reached Rome and the Apostolic See rather than that permission of far-reaching consequence would be granted to these jealous people of Cologne to pass judgment. Since Rome has the most learned people among the cardinals, Reuchlin's case will at least be considered more favorably there than those jealous people of Cologne—those beginners in grammar!—would ever allow. They are unable to distinguish between what an author [only] reports and what he himself believes; they cannot even understand what he says, or—I should more correctly say—they do not want to understand it. Farewell and pray for me, and let us pray for our Reuchlin.[4]

In this letter, Luther clearly sides with Reuchlin but also hints at the fact that he has adopted Reuchlin's use of Hebrew literature ("what the author reports and what he believes"). Luther will clarify this position later in *Born a Jew*, but his intention is clear, Jewish literature could be used to gain important philologic and grammatical insights into the Old Testament without adopting Jewish exegetical insights.[5] Knowledge of Jewish exegesis would also help further, Reuchlin

---

4 *LW* 48: 10. This was not Luther's first letter to Spalatin concerning Reuchlin. He first wrote in February. That letter will be discussed below.
5 Reuchlin, *Recommendation Whether to Confiscate, Destroy, and Burn All Jewish Book*, 66: "The [Jewish books] explain precisely how every word of the Bible is to be understood in the particularity of its linguistic context."

argued, the conversion of Jews to Christianity.[6] Luther, too, believed that knowledge of Jewish literature would aid in conversion. In 1521, in a collection of sermons on the Magnificat, he notes his hope for the future conversion of the Jews and remarks that because Christians have been both unchristian themselves and cruel to Jews it is perhaps no surprise that they have not converted. He ends his remarks with perhaps his most permissive view regarding Jews who would not convert: "let them be."[7]

The joint initiatives of increasing kindness to the Jews and holding out conversion were both expanded upon in the treatise *Born of the Jews.* Following Luther's appearance at the Diet of Worms and his subsequent disappearance, he became the subject of many and varied rumors. Some claimed that he had been secretly captured and killed. Even after he returned to Wittenberg in March 1522, he continued to be the subject of rumor. One of the more persistent rumors was that he was preaching and teaching heresy regarding the Virgin Mary and the conception of Christ. According to the rumor, Luther taught that "Jesus was conceived of the seed of Joseph and that Mary was not a virgin, but had many sons after Christ."[8] Luther initially regarded such rumors as ridiculous, but at the Diet, Charles V's younger brother, the Archduke Ferdinand, had repeated the rumor and asserted that it was true. When he received reports of the archduke's opinion in early 1523, he knew that he had to respond.[9] He began to write *That Jesus Christ was Born a Jew* almost immediately. We do not know exactly when it was finished but he tended to be a very fast writer, even more so when angry or under threat. If he began the treatise soon after a letter to Spalatin in January in which

---

6 Ibid., 67: "I also maintain, and have the sources to back me up, that if our clerics and exegetes of the Holy Scripture truly wish to win out in their debates with those of divergent faith, they had best familiarize themselves with such commentaries."

7 *WA* 7: 601.

8 *LW* 45: 197.

9 *WABR* 3: 19; Martin Luther, *Luther's Correspondence*, ed. Preserved Smith and Charles M. Jacobs, trans. Preserved Smith and Charles M. Jacobs, 2 vols. (Philadelphia: Lutheran Publication Society, 1913–1918), 165: ". . . a charge Ferdinand has openly made against me at Nuremberg, viz., that I teach the new doctrine that Christ is of the seed of Abraham. At first I took this charge as a jest, but they are so insistent on it that I have been compelled to believe it is true."

he declared his intention to respond then it is likely the treatise was published in the Spring of 1523.

The treatise is divided into two roughly equal parts. The first part defends the traditional doctrines of the Church regarding the miraculous conception of Jesus by the gift of the Holy Spirit. The second part is often said to be about Jews, but that is not entirely correct. The subject is not Jews, per se, but rather a refutation of Jewish perspectives on the Messiah and an explanation of why and how Old Testament literature regarding the Messiah leads to one and only one correct conclusion—that Jesus was the Messiah proclaimed in Hebrew scriptures.[10] He says at one point, "It is true that the Jews long ago began to feel the pressure of this might flood of evidence, and have anxiously defended their position with all manner of preposterous glosses."[11] Once he has demonstrated why the rabbi's glosses are preposterous and erroneous, he believes that Jews will finally "come along." Nevertheless, he says, "they have been led astray for so long and so far that one must deal gently with them, as people who have been all to strongly."[12]

He then moves into the two most often cited paragraphs of the 1523 treatise. In those two paragraphs, he explains why he advocates dealing gently with Jews. "Instead of this we are trying only to drive them by force, slandering them . . . So long as we treat them like dogs, how can we expect to work any good among them? . . . If we really want to help them, we must be guided in our dealings with them not by papal law but by Christian love. We must receive them cordially." He ends by echoing his statement in 1521, "If some of them should prove stiff-necked, what of it? After all, we ourselves are not all good Christians either."[13]

Often, this 1523 treatise has been used to argue that Luther once had a positive view of the Jews and then later in life turned violently and viciously against them. For example, Timothy Lull writes in the *Cambridge Companion to Martin Luther*, "Luther's first major writing about the Jews was a hopeful breakthrough in Christian

---

10 *LW* 45: 228: "Now let someone tell me: Where will one find a prince, or Messiah, or king, with whom all this accords so perfectly, as with our Lord Jesus Christ? Scripture and history agree so completely with one another that the Jews have nothing they can say to the contrary."
11 *LW* 45: 222.
12 *LW* 45: 229.
13 *LW* 45: 229.

reflections: *That Jesus Christ was Born a Jew* . . . Luther criticized the shameful treatment of Jews through the centuries and urged a new beginning guided by love . . . Much later Luther's attitude toward the Jews became more hostile."[14] Both of these statements are true, but the Luther's attitude toward the Jews did not undergo a fundamental change. Instead, what changed was his reaction to those who refused to convert. His tendency to view Jews only in terms of their possible conversion to Christianity did not change. At no time in his life did he regard Jews as worthy members of the community in their own right. In the 1520s, we see evidence of Luther's hope that his new reading of scripture would free both the Jew and the Christian from the shackles of erroneous exegesis. Thus freed from the bondage of history, Jews and Christians would embrace true Christianity.[15] As time went on, Luther became less and less optimistic. His pessimism ultimately turned to rage.

JEWS BECOMING BOTHERSOME: LUTHER AND THE JEWS IN THE LATE 1530s

In 1537, Luther received a letter from Josel of Rosheim. Josel was once given the appellation, "Chief of the Jews in the German Empire," and in the 1520s and early 1530s had corresponded with Luther on cordial, even friendly terms. He wrote to Luther in 1537 because he hoped that Luther might intercede with the Saxon elector John Frederick on his behalf. John Frederick had recently issued a

---

14 Timothy Lull, "Luther's Writings," in Donald McKim, ed., *Cambridge Companion to Martin Luther* (Cambridge: Cambridge University Press, 2003), 57.

15 See, for example, his letter to the converted Jew Bernard in May 1523, "But I think the cause of this ill-repute is not so much the Jews' obstinancy and wickedness, as rather their absurd and asinine ignorance and the wicked and shameless life of popes, priests, monks and universities. They give the Jews not a single spark of light or warmth, either in doctrine or in Christian life, but, on the contrary, they alienate the Jews' hearts and consciences by the darkness and the errors of their own traditions and by examples of the worst possible morals, and only impart to them the name of Christian . . . They find fault with the Jews because they only pretend to be converted, but they do not find fault with themselves because they only pretend to convert them ; nay, they seduce them from one error into another that is worse." Luther, *Luther's Correspondence*, 2.186.

proclamation calling for the expulsion of all Jews from Saxony. Luther learned of Josel's appeal via a letter from Wolfgang Capito.[16] We have both his letter back to Josel and a record of his immediate reaction after reading Capito's letter. His immediate reaction is in a Table Talk recorded by a former student, "A letter was delivered to Dr. Martin from a certain Jew [Josel] who requested and pleaded (as he had often written to the doctor before) that permission be obtained from the elector to grant him [Josel] safe entrance into and passage through the elector's principality. Dr. Martin responded, 'Why should these rascals, who injure people in body and property and who withdraw many Christians to their superstitions, be given permission [to enter or stay in Saxony]? In Moravia they have circumcised many Christians and call them by the new name of Sabbatarians . . . I'll write this Jew not to return.'" When Luther wrote to Josel, he was equally harsh and his frustration with increasingly (as he saw them) bothersome Jews is apparent:

My dear Josel:

I would have gladly interceded for you, both orally and in writing, before my gracious lord [the elector], just as my writings have greatly served the whole of Jewry. But because your people so shamefully misuse this service of mine and undertake things that we Christians simply shall not bear from you, they themselves have robbed me of all the influence I might otherwise have been able to exercise before princes and lords on your behalf.

For my opinion was, and still is, that one should treat the Jews in a kindly manner, that God may perhaps look graciously upon them and bring them to their Messiah—but not so that through my good will and influence they might be strengthened in their error and become still more bothersome.

I propose to write a pamphlet about this if God gives me space and time, to see if I cannot win some from your venerable tribe of the patriarchs and prophets and bring them to your promised Messiah.[17]

It is unclear whether or not Luther's next treatise *Against the Sabbatarians* was the treatise that he spoke of to Josel. The case is

---

16 *WABR* 8: 76 (Br. n. 3152).
17 *LW* 47: 62.

compelling if only because *Sabbatarians* was penned in the weeks following his letter to Josel and because he connected Josel's request to the Sabbatarians when he first read Capito's letter.

Against the Sabbatarians, whether it is the intended treatise, was written because Luther had heard of a group of people, called Sabbatarians, who advocated a strict observance of the Old Testament Law and strictly observed the Sabbath on Saturday (thus the name). These Sabbatarians were Christians, but Luther believed that they had been encouraged to observe the Law by Jews. We have no evidence that this is true. It is just as likely, as with Anabaptists, that this small Christian sect arrived at these theological commitments by themselves. Nevertheless, because Luther believed that Jews and rabbis were responsible for the sect, he discusses them at length in the treatise and it marks a significant step in Luther's relationship to Jews.

The quiet patience he advocated in 1523 is now entirely gone as the very first line of *Sabbatarians* makes clear: "Because of their rabbis, the Jewish people have become very stubborn and are therefore very difficult to win over."[18] Luther's early hope that droves of Jews would convert to Christianity has all but disappeared and in its place anger at rabbis has grown. One of the reasons for his anger was a developing belief that the rabbis were intentionally misleading (he uses the word blinding) people (both their own community and the Sabbatarians) through their interpretation of scripture. Thus, *Sabbatarians* contains a section in which he used his knowledge of Hebrew to argue against the rabbis' interpretation of *le-olam*,[19] which was an important Hebrew word in Jewish/Christian debates over whether or not the Law of Moses continued to apply to Christians. Luther writes,

> But when the Jews bandy about the word *le-olam* to prove their point, quoting Moses' command to keep such and such laws which he gave them *le-olam*, that is "eternally," these rascals are well aware that this is empty talk designed to dupe those not versed in the Hebrew language. They would not dare to confront me or anyone else who understands a little Hebrew with this, unless to make a joke or to provoke some laughter.[20]

---

18 *WA* 50: 312. *Against the Sabbatarians* is translated in *LW* 47: 65–98.
19 He thereby gave testimony to the position he took during the Reuchlin-Pfefferkorn debate over the use of Hebrew in apologetics and evangelism.
20 *LW* 47: 81.

Luther uses the rest of the treatise to argue that Jewish perversity in exegesis leads them, in his opinion, to the inescapable position that they must be right and "God must ever be a liar."[21] Their obstinacy, he believed, resulted in fifteen hundred years of exile and abuse. He urges them to return to the faith of their ancestors—which he believed was a faith in the Messiah. That faith has been made known in Jesus Christ. They reject this, however, and to Luther reveal themselves to be a "wicked people who glory solely in the boast that they are Abraham's seed."[22] His belief that Jews were no longer just stubborn but wicked would only grow when he read Anton Margaritha's *Der ganze jüdische Glaube* (The Whole Jewish Faith) in 1539.

Margaritha, like Pfefferkorn, was a Jewish convert to Christianity. Following his conversion, he taught Hebrew at a number of German universities finally ending up at Vienna. In 1530, he wrote *The Whole Jewish Faith.* In *Jewish Faith*, he describes the spiritual and prayer life of Jewish communities. Josel of Augsburg vehemently contested Margaritha's portrayal of some anti-Christian sentiments attributed to Jews in Margaritha, but Luther seems to have believed them. The most important section for Luther's view of the Jews comes near the end of the treatise when Margaritha discusses the *Aleinu* ("It is our duty") prayer that comes at the end of the service of Rosh Hashanah. The prayer thanks God for giving Israel a special calling and notes that Jews have a "duty" to praise Adonai (the Lord) as the one true God. None of this, in itself was new or controversial. What was controversial was Margaritha's contention that ten extra words were inserted into the prayer to mock Christians. The ten words state, "These words read [in Hebrew] *Shehem korim umistachevim le hevel vorik umispallelim le el lo joschia*, that is, they kneel and bow to a foolishness and vanity and pray to a god that cannot help. And when they pray these ten words, they spit three times against Christ and his believers."[23] Margaritha used a complex system of assigning a number to each Hebrew Letter (similar to Cabala) in order to prove that

---

21 *LW* 47: 88.

22 *LW* 47: 96 (translation altered).

23 Anton Margaritha, *Der Ganze Jüdische Glaube* (Augsburg: Heynrich Steyner, 1530), V4r. A complete English translation (from which the above is taken) of the *Aleinu* prayer section can be found in Michael T. Walton, "Anthonius Margaritha: Honest Reporter?," *Sixteenth Century Journal* 36/1 (2005).

the words "foolishness and vanity" add up to mean Jeschua or Jesus. Thus one could translate the sentence according to Margaritha, "they bow to Jesus and pray to a god that cannot help." Margaritha also noted that in many copies of the service there is space left blank on the page to fill in the missing ten words so that they will escape the eye of Christian censors when books containing the service were printed. Finally, Margaritha referred to a Medieval Jewish polemic work against Christians *Toledot Yeshu* that argues that Jesus was born illegitimately and gained control over the ineffable name of God (YHWH) in order to work his supposed miracles. All of these points seemed to confirm for Luther that Jews had no intention of converting to Christianity, that they lied to and deceived Christians, and that they actively participated in blasphemy. These three beliefs would drive Luther to his final and lasting perspective of Jews.

ON THE JEWS AND THEIR LIES—LUTHER AND THE JEWS IN THE 1540s

In the 1540s, Martin Luther would pen two important tracts on Jews: discuss the use of Hebrew in a treatise on the Last Words of David, and on the night before he died preach against Jews and call for their expulsion from Eisleben. Of these four writings, the 1543 *On the Jews and Their Lies* is the longest and most famous (see Figure 9.1).

It is apparent immediately in *Jews and Their Lies* that Luther has abandoned all hope in converting Jews to Christianity. On the very first page of the treatise he makes his views on this point very clear, "Much less do I propose to convert the Jews, for that is impossible."[24] He has also, by this point, abandoned his belief that engagement and dialog will bring about conversion, "do not engage much in debate with Jews about the articles of our faith. From their youth they have been so nurtured with venom and rancor against our Lord that there is not hope until they reach the point where their misery finally makes them pliable and they are forced to confess that the Messiah has come and that he is our Jesus."[25] For nearly 100 pages, Luther then reports on various lies he believes have been spread by Jews. He adopts a number of common Medieval fears about Jews (such as they secretly seek to kill all Christians)[26] and then advocates a "harsh mercy" that will finally

---

24 *LW* 47: 137.
25 *LW* 47: 139.
26 *LW* 47: 267.

Figure 9.1 Coverpage, *On the Jews and Their Lies*; Martin Luther, *Von den Jüden und ihren lügen* (Wittenberg, 1543). Reprinted by permission of the Bayerische Staatsbibliothek, Munich.

end Jewish blasphemy and bring the Jews to the level of misery needed to enable their conversion.[27] Luther's harsh mercy had seven steps:

1. First, to set fire to their synagogues or schools and to bury and cover with dirt whatever will not burn, so that no man will ever

27 *LW* 47: 268. Martin Bertram translates Luther's phrase, "scharffe barmherzigkeit" as "sharp mercy." This is an exact literal translation, but I prefer Heiko Oberman's rendition of "harsh mercy," for that conveys Luther's intention more accurately. Oberman, however, is incorrect when he states that the phrase is left out of modern translations. It is there, just not translated as Oberman would have liked. See, Oberman, *Luther: Man between God and the Devil*, 290.

again see a stone or cinder of them. This is to be done in honor of our Lord and of Christendom, so that God might see that we are Christians, and do not condone or knowingly tolerate such public lying, cursing, and blaspheming of his Son and of his Christians. For whatever we tolerated in the past unknowingly—and I myself was unaware of it—will be pardoned by God. But if we, now that we are informed, were to protect and shield such a house for the Jews, existing right before our very nose, in which they lie about, blaspheme, curse, vilify, and defame Christ and us (as was heard above), it would be the same as if we were doing all this and even worse ourselves, as we very well know.[28]

2. Second, I advise that their houses also be razed and destroyed. For they pursue in them the same aims as in their synagogues. Instead they might be lodged under a roof or in a barn, like the gypsies. This will bring home to them the fact that they are not masters in our country, as they boast, but that they are living in exile and in captivity, as they incessantly wail and lament about us before God.[29]

3. Third, I advise that all their prayer books and Talmudic writings, in which such idolatry, lies, cursing, and blasphemy are taught, be taken from them.[30]

4. Fourth, I advise that their rabbis be forbidden to teach henceforth on pain of loss of life and limb.[31]

5. Fifth, I advise that safe-conduct on the highways be abolished completely for the Jews. For they have no business in the country-side, since they are not lords, officials, tradesmen, or the like. Let them stay at home.[32]

6. Sixth, I advise that usury be prohibited to them, and that all cash and treasure of silver and gold be taken from them and put aside for safekeeping. The reason for such a measure is that, as said above, they have no other means of earning a livelihood than usury, and by it they have stolen and robbed from us all they possess. Such money should now be used in no other way than the

---

28 *LW* 47: 268–9.

29 *LW* 47: 269.

30 *LW* 47: 269. The irony in this statement, in that he has know come full circle and adopted the position of Jacob von Hockstraten, should not be lost.

31 *LW* 47: 269.

32 *LW* 47: 270.

following: Whenever a Jew is sincerely converted, he should be handed one hundred, two hundred, or three hundred florins, as personal circumstances may suggest.[33]

7. Seventh, I recommend putting a flail, an ax, a hoe, a spade, a distaff, or a spindle into the hands of young, strong Jews and Jewesses and letting them earn their bread in the sweat of their brow, as was imposed on the children of Adam (Gen. 3 [.19]). For it is not fitting that they should let us accursed Goyim toil in the sweat of our faces while they, the holy people, idle away their time behind the stove, feasting and farting, and on top of all, boasting blasphemously of their lordship over the Christians by means of our sweat. No, one should toss out these lazy rogues by the seat of their pants.[34]

Those seven points are perhaps the most disturbing paragraphs in all of Luther's massive corpus and it is easy to sympathize with Roland Bainton's wish that "Luther had died before ever this tract was written."[35] It is a bit of hyperbole to state that *On the Jews* provided the blueprint for Kristallnacht, it is however, difficult to read one of the opening lines of his next treatise without thinking of the Holocaust, "Even if they were punished in the most gruesome manner that the streets ran with blood, that their dead would be counted, not in the hundreds of thousands but in the millions."[36]

That chilling line comes from the last major tract that Luther wrote on the Jews was written almost immediately after *On the Jews* and continues its tone and tenor from the first page onward. The tract is not directed to Jews or to their possible conversion, as in *On the Jews* he has abandoned that hope entirely.[37] Instead, *Vom Schem*

---

33 *LW* 47: 270.

34 *LW* 47: 272.

35 Bainton, *Here I Stand: A Life of Martin Luther*, 379.

36 The statement about Kristallnacht comes from Dairmaid MacCulloch, *Reformation: Europe's House Divided, 1490–1700.* (New York: Penguin, 2004), 666–7. The quotation is from, Martin Luther and Gerhard Falk, *The Jew in Christian Theology: Martin Luther's Anti-Jewish Vom Schem Hamphoras, Previously Unpublished in English*, trans. Gerhard Falk (Jefferson, NC: McFarland & Co., 1992), 167.

37 "A Jew or a Jewish heart is as hard as stone and iron and cannot be moved by any means. Even if Moses and all the Prophets came and did all their wonderous works in front of their eyes as did Christ and his apostles, so that they would quit their unreason, it would still be useless."

Hamphoras was written to warn Christians of Jewish "lies" that he did not cover in *On the Jews*. The title of the work means *On the Ineffable Name* and refers to the Tetragrammaton YHWH or Yahweh, one of the Old Testament names for God. From Margaritha, Luther learned of the Jewish story that Jesus gained control of the Name of God and was therefore able to perform miracles and deceive people. In *Ineffable Name*, Luther translated a section of a fourteenth century tract by a Carthusian monk, Salvagus Porchetus, that purported to accurately convey the contents of the anti-Christian legend. After Luther printed his translation, he went through it point by point to show its historical, theological, and biblical inaccuracies. His criticisms and vulgar language, however, were too much for many Christians. Martin Bullinger wrote from Zurich that Luther's tract was swinish and filthy, "If this had been written by a swineherd, rather than by a celebrated shepherd of souls, it might have some, but very little, justification."[38]

Luther finished *Ineffable Name* sometime in March 1543 and then almost immediately turned to discuss the Last Words of David from 2 Samuel 23. The angry polemicist is almost completely gone from this work. There are no pogroms called for in this treatise. What does become apparent, however, is the degree to which Luther's disappointment in the lack of Jewish conversion and anger therein has bled over into his scholarship. Almost completely gone is the scholar who wrote George Spalatin in 1514 and praised the work of Reuchlin. Then, he supported the use of rabbis in discerning the literal or grammatical meaning of a Hebrew word when translating. Now he regrets such dependence, "their [rabbis'] opinion would not impel me to learn a single letter of the Hebrew language. The reason for that is this: We Christians have the meaning and import of the Bible because we have the New Testament, that is, Jesus Christ, who was promised in the Old Testament and who later appeared and brought with Him the light and the true meaning of Scripture."[39] His distain for Hebrew learning and his drive to find a Christological interpretation

---

Vom Schem Hamphoras is not included in the *LW*. This translation is taken from, Luther and Falk, *Martin Luther's Vom Schem Hamphoras*, 167. Falk also helpfully provides the German version as well. *Vom Schem Hamphoras* can also be found in *WA* 53: 579–648.

38 *WA* 53: 574. ET in Eric Gritsch, *Martin—God's Court Jester: Luther in Retrospect* (Philadelphia: Fortress Press, 1983), 144.

39 *LW* 15: 267.

in the words of David are so strong that at one point he forces 1 Chronicles 17.17 to read, "thou has regarded me as in the form of a Man who is God the Lord on high."[40] Earlier, he had translated that same sentence as "And you Lord God have considered me as a man above all others."[41]

Luther's frustration with Jews and his belief that they represented a malevolent influence on German society also spilled over into his personal life. In the last month of his life, he traveled to Eisleben to mediate a dispute there. On the way to Eisleben, he suffered the first of what would be multiple heart attacks over the next two weeks. In a letter written that evening to his wife, Katherine Luther, he first minimizes the events of the day saying only that he felt "dizzy." But then he goes on to contemplate whether or not Jews were responsible for his attack:

> Yes, on the way, shortly before Eisleben, I became dizzy. That was my fault. Had you been here, however, you would have said that it was the fault of the Jews or their god. For shortly before Eisleben we had to travel through a village in which many Jews are living, [and] perhaps they have attacked me so painfully. At this time over fifty Jews reside here in the city of Eisleben. It is true that when I passed by the village such a cold wind blew from behind into the carriage and on my head through the beret, [that it seemed] as if it intended to turn my brain to ice. This might have helped me somewhat to become dizzy . . . After the main issues have been settled, I have to start expelling the Jews. Count Albrecht is hostile to them and has already outlawed them. But no one harms them as yet. If God grants it I shall aid Count Albrecht from the pulpit, and outlaw them too.[42]

Luther would not have the opportunity to preach against the Jews in Eisleben. He was struck again by another heart attack and so he was prevented from preaching. Instead, he most likely dictated an addendum to his final sermon in Eisleben (which was his final sermon ever) that he hoped would be read to the people. In that sermon addendum, he fulfilled his pledge to aid Albrecht in the expulsion of the Jews from Eisleben.

---

40 *LW* 15: 286.
41 *WA* 54: 20.
42 *LW* 50: 290.

In this addendum, he returns again to his fear that Jews "would kill us all if they could." He declares that the Jews are "our public enemies" who "blaspheme against Jesus Christ every day." As with all his other writings on the Jews, he does offer out the hand of welcome to those who convert, "if one converts, ceases his usury, and accepts Christ, then we will regard him as a brother." But, to those who do not convert, Luther advocates forceful expulsion from Eisleben, "the lords among you should not allow them to remain, but should drive them away."[43] He ends this short addendum or warning (*Warnung*) as he called it, by again holding out the possibility of forgiveness for those who converted or expulsion for those who did not.

EXCUSES AND EXPLANATIONS—LUTHER AND THE JEWS IN SCHOLARSHIP

There are roughly four lines of inquiry used to contextualize, explain, and in some cases excuse Luther's writings against the Jews. The first argues that Luther was a man of his times and not particularly different from many others in his fear and hatred of Jews. Desiderius Erasmus, Johannes Eck, and Martin Bucer were all anti-Jewish, though none were as virulent as Luther. The second perspective argues that Luther wrote in equally harsh terms against the peasants during the Peasants' War and against Anabaptists. This, too, is also true. The third position is common to many topics within Luther studies and that is to contrast the young ebullient and vigorous Luther with an embittered and sick old man. The final standpoint argues that Luther's anti-Jewish literature must be distinguished from the later anti-Semitism that culminated in the Nazi Holocaust.

Points one and two are both valid and historically accurate but neither paints a complete picture. For the most part, anti-Jewish literature was rare in the sixteenth century and was sometimes even condemned. For example, Rabbi Josel succeeded in having Margaritha's work condemned by the emperor himself in 1530. Likewise, in 1540 Andreas Osiander—the Lutheran pastor of Nuremberg, preached against the Jewish "blood-libel," which is the charge that Jews ritually murdered Christian Children.[44] Those sermons were subsequently published by

---

43 *WA* 51: 195.
44 See Joy Kammerling, "Andreas Osiander's Sermons on the Jews," in *Lutheran Quarterly* 15/1 (2001): 59–84.

a grateful Jewish community. Thus, not everyone in the sixteenth century was unabashedly anti-Jewish. It was common, certainly, but it was possible to look beyond the stereotypes.

The final two positions are far more important because they provide an excuse by way of explanation. Mark Edwards in *Luther's Last Battles* does an excellent job of highlighting the many and varied ways in which the young and vibrant Luther is contrasted against the aged and calcified Luther. In the end, he finds this dichotomy to be unsupportable. Since his work in the 1980s, John Maxfield has produced a detailed study of Luther's work as a university lecturer on the book of Genesis. In *Luther's Lectures on Genesis* a portrait of a man in absolute control of his faculties emerges. The Luther painted by Maxfield is not a decrepit and decaying man subject to violent outbursts that border on dementia. Rather, Luther is portrayed as an engaged scholar who daily sought to shape and hone his students for the work of building up the church. Thus, as tempting as it might be to excuse Luther's later writings as the rantings of a sickly old man, that thesis simply cannot be sustained. The "Late Luther" was also a "vigorous Luther."

Finally, the most common explanation/excuse of Luther's anti-Jewish writings is to differentiate between the anti-Semitism of the Nazi era and Luther's anti-Judaism. The Third Reich's anti-Semitism saw Jews as a foreign race of people that threatened the purity of the German nation. They viewed Jews in racial categories and it did not matter whether or not one was a Christian of Jewish descent or not. In contrast, according to some, Luther looked at Jews as theological adversaries but did not view them as a race of people. Heiko Oberman writes, "one must realize that Luther does not see 'a race' when he looks at the Jews, nor are baptized and unbaptized Jews for Luther the exponents of an ethnic, racial unit. Baptized Jews belong unqualifiedly to the people of God, just as do baptized Germans, the Gentiles."[45] It is certainly true that no one in the sixteenth century viewed Jews in the same racial categories as the Nazis did four centuries later. If sixteenth-century people did speak of races they were most often speaking of what we would today call ethnicities, thus Germans were a "race," Italians another. It is also

---

45 Heiko Augustinus Oberman, *The Roots of Anti-Semitism in the Age of Renaissance and Reformation*, trans. James I Porter (Philadelphia: Fortress, 1984), 102.

true that generally Luther did regard baptized Jews as complete members of their new community. On the other hand, Luther did look at Jewish communities as a collective whole that he viewed with suspicion, fear, and sometimes loathing. It must also be asked whether or not it really matters to minority communities why they are being persecuted. Whether one persecutes them for their religion or their ethnicity, the expulsions are still expulsions and the prohibitions on what one might do for work or where one might live are still prohibitions. Whether Luther called for their synagogues to be burned because they were a race or a religion matters little to people who watch flames flicker.

LUTHER AND HITLER

In the chapter on Martin Luther and politics, we discussed the supposed relationship between Luther's theology and a perceived German predisposition for totalitarian government. Here we turn to Luther's theology and Hitler's anti-Semitism. In 1946, at his post-World War II trial in Nuremberg, the Nazi propagandist Julius Streicher defended the anti-Semitic nature of his newspaper when he was questioned by his lawyer:

> Anti-Semitic publications have existed in Germany for centuries. A book I had [owned] was written by Martin Luther, it was confiscated . . . In the book, *The Jews and Their Lies*, Dr. Martin Luther writes that Jews are a serpent's brood and one should burn down their synagogues and destroy them.[46]

At that point, Streicher's lawyer interrupted him and sought to keep him from making small speeches before the Tribunal's judges. Nevertheless, Streicher had made his point. The great German hero, Dr. Martin Luther, was as anti-Semitic as any Nazi and that Streicher's newspaper, *Der Stürmer*, was no different than Luther's treatise on the Jews. Peter Wiener, writing before the worst examples of the Holocaust were completely known, went even farther. "He

---

46 *Trial of the Major War Criminals before the International Military Tribunal, Nuremberg 14 Nov 1945–1 Oct 1946: Official English Language Translation*, 42 vols. (Nuremberg, Germany: International Military Tribunal, 1947), 318.

[Luther] preached and practised a violent antisemitism and extermination of the Jews which remain unsurpassed even by Hitler."[47] The American journalist William L. Shirer essentially agreed with Streicher and Wiener: "He [Luther] wanted Germany rid of the Jews . . . and furthermore, 'that their synagogues or schools be set on fire, that their houses be broken up and destroyed . . .'—advice that was literally followed four centuries later by Hitler, Goering, and Himmler."[48] Uwe Siemon-Netto in *The Fabricated Luther* has argued passionately that such a connection between Martin Luther and Adolf Hitler represents a simplistic cliché and has little historical accuracy beyond making a sensationalist headline.[49] There are literally hundreds of articles, websites, and books dedicated to examining the relationship between Martin Luther and the Nazis with people often coming down on one side of the debate or the other. In the end, Franklin Sherman, the editor and translator of Luther's *On the Jews and Their Lies* in the American *Luther's Works*, is probably the closest to the truth when he writes, "It would of course be an anachronism to apply the *term* 'antisemitism' to Luther, since it was only invented in the nineteenth century. But neither can it be maintained that Luther's writings against the Jews are merely a set of cool, calm, collected theological judgments. His writings are full of rage, and indeed hatred, against *an identifiable human group*, not just against a religious point of view; its against that group that his action proposals are directed. Luther cannot be distanced completely from modern antisemites. Regarding Luther's treatise *On the Jews and Their Lies*, Karl Jaspers was close to the mark when he exclaimed, '*Da steht das ganze Programm der Nazi Zeit schon*' ('There you already have the whole Nazi program') I would qualify this only by saying: the Nazi program down to and including *Kristallnacht*; but

---

47 Peter F. Wiener, *Martin Luther: Hitler's Spiritual Ancestor* (London: Hutchinson, 1945), 51. The pamphlet was originally written in 1942 as an anti-German pamphlet in England. See also, Gordon Rupp's response to Wiener, Gordon Rupp, *Martin Luther: Hitler's Cause or Cure* (London: Lutterworth, 1945).

48 William L. Shirer, *The Rise and Fall of the Third Reich: A History of Nazi Germany* (New York: Simon & Schuster, 1959), 236.

49 Uwe Siemon-Netto, *The Fabricated Luther: Refuting Nazi Connections and Other Modern Myths*, 2nd ed. (St. Louis: Concordia, 2007).

not the decision for genocide. Luther warned, even in his severest recommendations, 'you must not harm their persons.'"[50]

CONCLUSION

Carter Lindberg in his article on Martin Luther in a collection of essays on significant figures in history that have been accused of anti-Semitism, *Tainted Greatness*, makes the point that Luther's writings against Jews should be rejected because at their heart they reject Luther's own core theological commitments and "embraced the messianic pretensions of a theology of glory."[51] For Luther, any theology that viewed human works as necessary for the building up of the Kingdom of God was a theology of glory or a theology that glorified the work of people over the work of God. Instead Luther believed that the Kingdom of God was just that, God's Kingdom that would be fashioned and built by God. Too often, however, human beings are uncomfortable with allowing God to be God and instead seek to take on God's prerogatives in this world. Luther's frustration and anger with Jews was primarily a reaction to their rejection of his call to conversion. He believed that because he had stripped away centuries of false teachings that had encrusted the Gospel, Jews would flock to Christianity. They did not. In his frustration, then, he did fail to take seriously his theology and did not remain consistent with what he wrote to George Spalatin in 1514 that the conversion of Jews, "will be a work of God alone operating from within and not a work of man working—or rather playing—from without." Over the decades that followed, Luther came to believe that the conversion of the Jews was a work for him to complete and when they did not convert he regarded that as a direct rejection of himself.

Perhaps, like Noah's drunkenness, Luther's remarks in *On the Jews and Their Lies* can serve as a reminder that it is best to remember that even great men and women are fallible. Even the man who could

---

50 Franklin Sherman, "Steps Along the Way," in *Faith Transformed: Christian Encounters with Jews and Judaism*, ed. John C. Merkle (Collegeville: MN: A Michael Glazier Book published by The Liturgical Press, 2003), 63–4.

51 Carter Lindberg, "Tainted Greatness: Luther's Attitudes towards Judaism and Their Historical Reception," in *Tainted Greatness: Anti-Semitism and Cultural Heroes*, ed. Nancy A. Harrowitz (Philadelphia: Temple University Press, 1994), 28.

write *That Jesus was Born a Jew* could years later write *On the Jews*. We do best, then, to laud those in the past (or even the present) when they lift the human spirit and condemn them when they fall, fail, and give into the lesser angels of our nature. Ultimately, there can be no excuse for Luther's comments. They were inexcusable in 1545 and they remain inexcusable in 2010. The ethics of how one ought to engage others does not change with the hands of time. If it is wrong to call for another's house of worship to be destroyed today, it was wrong then regardless of the explanation. Perhaps Luther would be displeased with our assessment of his culpability today. But so, too, might Noah have complained to Luther about Luther's assessment of his behavior. But as his earlier comments in *Born a Jew* make clear, Luther knew that vitriolic attacks were not only inappropriate but unhelpful. In the end, the only lesson that we can draw from *Lies* is that we must remain constantly vigilant against any attempts to demonize one section of a population and we must admit that even the great can and do sometimes fall to great depths.

BIBLIOGRAPHY

This bibliography is meant to be neither exhaustive nor a recapitulation of the footnotes in each chapter. Rather, I have selected works that will help one continue one's research on each general topic. Those works marked by an asterisk "*" are excellent places to begin research.

LUTHER'S WRITTEN WORKS

Luther, M., *D. Martin Luthers Werke: Kritische Gesamtausgabe.* Weimar: H. Böhlau, 1883–1993.

*Luther, M., *Luther's Works.* St. Louis: Concordia; Philadelphia: Fortress Press, 1958–1986.

Luther, M., *Sermons of Martin Luther*, ed. John Nicholas Lenker, 8 vols. (1903–1909). Grand Rapids, MI: Baker, 1993.

Luther, M., *Luther on Women: A Sourcebook*, ed. and trans. S. Karant-Nunn and M. Wiesner-Hanks. Cambridge: Cambridge University Press, 2003.

BIOGRAPHIES OF LUTHER

*Bainton, R. H., *Here I Stand.* New York: Abingdon, 1950.

Bornkamm, H. *Luther in Mid-Career*, 1521–1530, ed. and with a Foreword by Karin Bornkamm, trans. from the German by E. Theodore Bachmann. Philadelphia: Fortress Press, 1983.

*Brecht, M., *Martin Luther*, trans. James L. Schaaf, 3 vols. Philadelphia: Fortress Press, 1985–1993 (German, 1981–1987).

Gritsch, E., *Martin—God's Court Jester: Luther in Retrospect.* Philadelphia: Fortress Press, 1983.

Kittelson, J. M., *Martin Luther: The Story of the Man and His Career.* Minneapolis: Fortress Press, 1986.

Köstlin, J., *The Life of Martin Luther*, trans. John G. Morris, 2 vols. Philadelphia: Lutheran Publication Society, 1883 (German, 1875).

Luther's Lives: Two Contemporary Accounts of Martin Luther, trans. and annotated by E. Vandiver, R. Keen, and T. Frazel. Manchester: Manchester University Press; New York: Palgrave, 2002.

*Oberman, H. A., *Luther: Man between God and the Devil*, trans. Eileen Walliser-Schwarzbart. New Haven, CT: Yale University Press, 1989 (German, 1982).

Schwiebert, E., *Luther: The Man and His Times*. St. Louis: Concordia, 1950.

GENERAL INTRODUCTIONS TO THE REFORMATION

Cameron, E., *The European Reformation*. Oxford: Clarendon Press, 1991.

*Lindberg, C., *The European Reformations*. 2nd edition. Oxford: Blackwell, 2009.

MacCulloch, D., *The Reformation*. New York: Penguin, 2003.

Ozment, S., *The Age of Reform: 1250–1550: An Intellectual and Religious History of Late Medieval and Reformation Europe*. New Haven: Yale University Press, 1980.

———. *Protestants: The Birth of a Revolution*. New York: Doubleday, 1992.

GENERAL INTRODUCTIONS TO LUTHER'S THOUGHT

Althaus, P., *The Theology of Martin Luther*, trans. Robert C. Schultz. Philadelphia: Fortress Press, 1966 (German, 1962).

Bornkamm, H., *Luther's World of Thought,* trans. from the German by Martin H. Bertram. St. Louis: Concordia, 1958.

Ebeling, G., *Luther: An Introduction to His Thought*, trans. R. A. Wilson. Philadelphia: Fortress Press, 1970 (German, 1964).

Köstlin, J., *The Theology of Martin Luther*, trans. Charles E. Hay. Philadelphia: Lutheran Publication Society, 1897 (German, 1863).

Lohse, B., *Martin Luther*, trans. Robert C. Schultz. Philadelphia: Fortress Press, 1986 (German, 1980).

*———. *Martin Luther's Theology: Its Historical and Systematic Development*, trans. Roy A. Harrisville. Minneapolis: Fortress Press, 1999 (German, 1995).

*McGrath, A., *The Intellectual Origins of the European Reformation*. Oxford: Blackwell Press, 1987.

———. *Reformation Thought: An Introduction*. 2nd edition. Cambridge, MA: Blackwell Press, 1993.

*McKim, D. ed., *Cambridge Companion to Martin Luther*. Cambridge: Cambridge University Press, 2003.

Pelikan, J., *The Christian Tradition: A History of the Development of Doctrine*. Volume 4: Reformation of Church and Dogma (1300–1700). Chicago: University of Chicago Press, 1984.

LUTHER AND JUSTIFICATION

Forde, G. O., *Justification by Faith: A Matter of Death and Life*. Philadelphia: Fortress Press, 1982.

Gerrish, B. A., *Grace and Reason: A Study in the Theology of Luther*. 1962. Reprint. Chicago: University of Chicago Press, 1979.

Grane, L., *Martinus Noster: Luther in the German Reform Movement, 1518–1521*. Mainz: Zabern, 1994.

Kärkkäinen, V., *One with God: Salvation as Deification and Justification*. Collegeville, MN: Liturgical Press, 2004. Please also be sure to consult, D. Whitford, "Review of *One with God*." *Reviews in Religion and Theology* 13/2 (2006): 185–7.

Mannermaa, T., *Christ Present in Faith*, trans. K. Stjerna. Minneapolis: Augsburg Fortress, 2005.

*McGrath, A., *Iustitia Dei: A History of the Doctrine of Justification*. 3rd edition. Cambridge: Cambridge University Press, 2005.

Oberman, H. A., *The Harvest of Medieval Theology: Gabriel Biel and Late Medieval Nominalism*. Cambridge, MA: Harvard University Press, 1963.

Pesch, O., "Free by Faith: Luther's Contribution to a Theological Anthropology," in *Martin Luther and the Modern Mind: Freedom, Conscience, Toleration, Rights*, ed. Manfred Hoffmann, pp. 23–60. Lewiston, NY: Edwin Mellen, 1985.

Saarnivaara, U., *Luther Discovers the Gospel: New Light upon Luther's Way from Medieval Catholicism to Evangelical Faith*. St. Louis: Concordia, 1951.

Zachman, R., *The Assurance of Faith: Conscience in the Theologies of Martin Luther and John Calvin*. Minneapolis: Fortress, 1993.

LAW, GOSPEL, AND THE THEOLOGY OF THE CROSS

Forde, G., *On Being a Theologian of the Cross: Reflections on Luther's Heidelberg Disputation, 1518*. Grand Rapids: Eerdmans, 1997.

*Loewenich, W., von. *Luther's Theology of the Cross*, trans. Herbert J. A. Bouman. Minneapolis: Augsburg, 1976.

McGrath, A., *Luther's Theology of the Cross: Martin Luther's Theological Breakthrough*. Oxford: Blackwell, 1985.

Watson, P., *Let God Be God*. London: Epworth Press, 1947.

THE BONDAGE OF THE WILL

Bainton, R., *Erasmus of Christendom*. New York: Scribner, 1969.

*Kolb, R., *Bound Choice, Election, and Wittenberg Theological Method: From Martin Luther to the Formula of Concord*. Grand Rapids, MI: Eerdmans, 2005.

Lohse, B., *Martin Luther's Theology: Its Historical and Systematic Development*. Minneapolis, MN: Fortress Press, 1999.

*McSorley, H., *Luther: Right or Wrong? An Ecumenical-Theological Study of Luther's Major Work, The Bondage of the Will*. New York: Newman, 1969.

Rupp, G. and P. Watson, eds., *Luther and Erasmus: Free Will and Salvation*. Philadelphia: Westminster Press, 1969.

Watson, P., *Let God Be God*. London: Epworth Press, 1947.

THE ANTICHRIST

Emmerson, R., *Antichrist in the Middle Ages: A Study of Medieval Apocalypticism, Art, and Literature*. Seattle, WA: University of Washington Press, 1981.

Hendrix, S., *Luther and the Papacy: Stages in a Reformation Conflict*. Philadelphia: Fortress, 1981.

Hughes, K. L., *Constructing Antichrist: Paul, Biblical Commentary, and the Development of Doctrine in the Early Middle Ages*. Washington, DC: Catholic University of America Press, 2005.

*McGinn, B., *Antichrist: Two Thousand Years of the Human Fascination with Evil*. New York: Columbia University Press, 1994.

*Oberman, H., "Teufelsdreck: Eschatology and Scatology in the 'Old' Luther," *Sixteenth Century Journal* 19/3 (1988): 434–50.

Preuss, H., *Vorstellungen vom Antichrist: im späteren Mittelalter, bei Luther und in der konfessionellen Polemik*. Leipzig: Hinrichs'sche Buchhandlung, 1906.

Russell, W. R., "Martin Luther's Understanding of the Pope as the Antichrist," *Archiv für Reformationsgeschichte* 85 (1994): 32–44.

Whitford, D., "The Papal Antichrist: Martin Luther and the Underappreciated Influence of Lorenzo Valla," *Renaissance Quarterly* 61/1 (2008): 26–52.

POLITICS

Allen, J. W., *A History of Political Thought in the Sixteenth Century*. London: Methuen Press, 1957.

Althaus, P., *The Ethics of Martin Luther*, trans. Robert C. Schultz. Philadelphia: Fortress Press, 1972.

*Cargill Thompson, W. D. J., *The Political Thought of Martin Luther*, ed. Philip Broadhead. Totowa, NJ: Barnes & Noble, 1984.

*Keen, R., *Divine and Human Authority in Reformation Thought: German Theologians on Political Order*, 1520–1555. Nieuwkoop: B. De Graaf, 1997.

Skinner, Q., *The Foundations of Modern Political Thought, 2: The Age of the Reformation*. Cambridge: Cambridge University Press, 1978.

Tonkin, J., *The Church and the Secular Order in Reformation Thought*. New York, Columbia University Press, 1971

Tracy, J., ed., *Luther and the Modern State in Germany*. Kirksville, MO: Sixteenth Century Journal Publishers, 1986.

PEASANTS' WAR

Baylor, M. G., *The Radical Reformation, Cambridge Texts in the History of Political Thought*. Cambridge: Cambridge University Press, 1991.

Blickle, P., *The Revolution of 1525. The German Peasants' War from a New Perspective*. Baltimore and London: The Johns Hopkins Press, 1981.

Kolb, R., "The Theologians and the Peasants: Conservative Evangelical Reaction to the German Peasant's Revolt," *Archiv für Reformationsgeschichte* 69 (1978): 103–31.

Müntzer, T. and P. Matheson., *The Collected Works of Thomas Müntzer.* Edinburgh: T&T Clark, 1988.

*Scribner, R., *For the Sake of Simple Folk. Popular Propaganda for the German Reformation.* Cambridge: Cambridge University Press, 1979.

*Stayer, J., *The German Peasants' War and the Anabaptist Community of Goods,* Montreal and Kingston: McGill University Press, 1991.

*Williams, G. H., *The Radical Reformation.* 3rd edition, *Sixteenth Century Essays & Studies; V. 15.* Kirksville, MO: Sixteenth Century Journal Publishers, 1992.

LUTHER AND THE JEWS

Edwards, M., *Luther's Last Battles: Politics and Polemics, 1531- 46.* Ithaca: Cornell University Press, 1983.

*———. "Toward an Understanding of Luther's Attacks on the Jews," in *Christians, Jews, and Other Worlds: Patterns of Conflict and Accommodation,* ed. P. Gallagher, pp. 1–19. London: University Press of America, 1988.

Gritsch, E., "Was Luther Anti-Semitic?" *Christian History* 12/3 (1993): 38–9.

*Lindberg, C., "Tainted Greatness: Luther's Attitudes toward Judaism and Their Historical Reception," in *Tainted Greatness: Antisemitism and Cultural Heroes,* ed. N. Harrowitz. Philadelphia: Temple University Press, 1994.

Luther, M., *The Jew in Christian Theology: Martin Luther's Anti-Jewish Vom Schem Hamphoras,* previously unpublished in English, trans. Gerhard Falk. Jefferson, NC: McFarland & Co., 1992. See also, Falk's introduction.

*Oberman, H., *The Roots of Antisemitism in the Age of Renaissance and Reformation,* trans. J. Porter. Philadelphia: Fortress, 1984.

Rowan, S., "Luther, Bucer and Eck on the Jews," *The Sixteenth Century Journal* 16/1 (1985): 79–90.

Rupp, G., *Martin Luther and the Jews.* London: Council of Christians and Jews, 1972.

Siemon-Netto, U., *The Fabricated Luther: Refuting Nazi Connections and Other Modern Myths.* 2nd edition. St. Louis: Concordia, 2007.

Wiener, P., *Martin Luther: Hitler's Spiritual Ancestor.* London: Hutchinson, 1945.

INDEX